HM TREASURY  Small Busine Service  'er ...mmunities

Enterprise and economic opportunity in deprived areas

A consultation on proposals for a Local Enterprise Growth Initiative

March 2005

The Government has adopted a code of practice on consultations. Though they have no legal force, and cannot prevail over statutory or other mandatory external requirements (e.g. under European Community Law), they should otherwise generally be regarded as binding on UK departments and their agencies, unless Ministers conclude that exceptional circumstances require a departure.

The full consultation code may be viewed at: www.cabinet-office.gov.co.uk/regulation/consultation/introduction.htm

Small Business Service contacts

This document can be accessed from the SBS internet site at:
www.sbs.gov.uk

For further information on the SBS and its work, contact:

SBS Enquiry Line
St Mary's House
c/o Moorfoot
Sheffield
S1 4PQ

Tel: 0114 259 7788
Fax: 0114 259 7330

E-mail: gatewayenquiries@sbs.gov.uk

Office of the Deputy Prime Minister contacts

This document can be accessed from the ODPM internet site at:
www.odpm.gov.uk

For further information on the ODPM and its work, contact:

ODPM Public Enquiries
Office of the Deputy Prime Minister
26 Whitehall
London
SW1A 2WH

Tel: 020 7944 4400

E-mail: enquiryodpm@odpm.gsi.gov.uk

HM Treasury contacts

This document can be accessed from the Treasury Internet site at:
www.hm-treasury.gov.uk

For further information on the Treasury and its work, contact:

Correspondence and Enquiry Unit
HM Treasury
1 Horse Guards Road
London
SW1A 2HQ

Tel: 020 7270 4558
Fax: 020 7270 4861

E-mail: ceu.enquiries@hm-treasury.gov.uk

ISBN: 1-84532-084-0

Printed by The Stationery Office   03/05   300790

CONTENTS

FOREWORD

Enterprise is the lifeblood of our economy – creating employment and prosperity, boosting productivity, and building sustainable communities. Our vision is to widen and deepen the enterprise culture in our country so that every woman and every man – regardless of background or community in which they live – has the chance to go as far as their talents and potential will take them, so that enterprise is truly open to all.

However, there is a persistent gap in levels of entrepreneurial activity between deprived areas and our most prosperous areas. If the highest rates of business activity in the UK were matched in deprived areas, there would be around an extra 160,000 businesses in the UK – and if the UK as a whole matched US enterprise rates there would be an extra 1.9 million businesses. In recent decades it was not businesses, but benefit offices that mushroomed in high unemployment communities.

Since 1997, the Government has introduced several measures to help promote enterprise in deprived areas – from the Phoenix Fund, the Community Investment Tax Relief, to Enterprise Areas. This British enterprise renaissance has been built upon our platform of economic stability – with the longest period of sustained economic growth for 200 years, interest rates at their lowest level for 30 years, and the longest period of low and stable inflation since the 1960s.

We believe Britain is now ready for the next round of enterprise reforms and a step-change in creating a more dynamic enterprise culture in our most deprived areas. We must ensure that there is no no-go area for enterprise in twenty-first century Britain.

But we cannot close this gap overnight, nor can Government do it alone. Success depends upon the innovation and creativity of both entrepreneurs and local communities themselves. Local authorities have a crucial role to play in tackling this challenge – sustainable communities depend on strong, effective local government that is well-led to deliver excellent services.

The Government therefore proposes to establish a Local Enterprise Growth Initiative (LEGI), worth £50 million in 2006-2007, rising to £150 million per year by 2008-2009, subject to confirmation in the 2006 Spending Review. The LEGI will help release the economic and productivity potential of our most deprived local areas through enterprise and investment – thereby boosting local incomes and employment opportunities, building sustainable communities and helping to overcome decades of disadvantage and poor economic performance.

This consultation document asks for your views on the details of this fund. We welcome your comments and look forward to building sustainable communities together.

John Healey MP

**Rt Hon
Nick Raynsford MP**

Nigel Griffiths MP

EXECUTIVE SUMMARY

I   The Government's central objective is to achieve high and stable levels of growth and employment. Previous publications have set-out the Government's strategy for raising productivity in the private sector and, within this, building an enterprise culture across the regions and localities of England. This document takes this analysis one step further by examining enterprise as a means of achieving sustainable economic development, growth and regeneration in some of the most deprived areas of the England – building on the Government's strategy for neighbourhood renewal.

2   Following this analysis, **the document consults on proposals for a Local Enterprise Growth Initiative (LEGI), worth £50 million in 2006-2007, rising to £150 million per year by 2008-2009, subject to confirmation in the 2006 Spending Review.** LEGI will operate in a devolved manner by supporting locally developed proposals to promote – and remove barriers to – enterprise in the most deprived areas of England.

THE ENTERPRISE VISION

3   Enterprise is one of the key drivers of the productivity of the UK economy. Building a strong enterprise culture and environment is vital in closing the productivity gap that exists between the UK and its main competitors.

4   The Government's vision is that anybody with the talent, potential and drive to succeed in business should have the opportunity and necessary support to do so, regardless of their background or where they live.

5   Therefore, the Government has a key role to play in ensuring the right conditions are in place for enterprise to flourish across the economy, both by building an enterprise friendly environment, and by correcting for specific market failures that create obstacles to successful enterprise.

ENTERPRISE IN DEPRIVED AREAS

6   At the local level, local authorities have a key role to play in developing the economies of local areas – working with their regional development agencies (RDAs) – to pursue their well-being power to promote the economic vitality of localities, as provided for in the Local Government Act 2000.

7   In particular, enterprise provides local authorities with a powerful means of pursuing sustainable economic development in deprived areas. Enterprise can contribute to the economic development of deprived areas through:

- local productivity growth;

- employment and income growth;

- improved local service provision;

- creating multiplier effects and building supply chains;

- increasing the local tax base;

- improving the physical environment; and

- investing in the community and building social capital.

8   Deprived areas can also present competitive advantages and opportunities for enterprise that are not always taken advantage of: often presenting a strategic location close to transport and communication links; untapped market demand; possibilities for clustering and multiplier effects; a pool of under-utilised labour; and often a significant commitment of public resources.

TACKLING THE ENTERPRISE GAP

9   However, levels of enterprise in deprived areas are significantly and persistently lower than in more affluent areas. Fewer businesses start-up in deprived areas and have a greater failure rate than in other areas.

10   Government should therefore intervene for two reasons:

1. **Efficiency**: local economies in deprived areas suffer from market failures that mean they are less efficient and productive than they could be.

2. **Equity**: concentrations of deprivation raise deep equity concerns in terms of sub-optimal outcomes for local people – from access to jobs, to health and crime.

11   While deprived areas often present competitive advantages and opportunities, they can also present significant barriers that are either more acute, or more persistent, than in more affluent areas. Barriers in deprived areas relate to: the ability of the entrepreneur or small business to access suitable finance and business support services; the lack of experience, skills or training of potential employees; a weak enterprise culture; a greater incidence of institutional or administrative barriers; and/or a poor business environment.

12   The Government therefore proposes three 'pillars' of support for enterprise in deprived areas:

1. **National**: tackling certain key enterprise development issues at the national level through an **ongoing commitment to build on the Enterprise Areas** package, where either economies of scale are required, or where issues are common across many areas.

2. **Regional**: devolving to the regional level new responsibilities for the delivery of **Business Link** and the **Phoenix Fund**, to enable an integrated approach to business support.

3. **Local**: building-on support through the Neighbourhood Renewal Strategy, providing significant commitment to support locally-appropriate plans for enterprise development through a **Local Enterprise Growth Initiative worth £50 million in 2006-2007, rising to £150 million per year by 2008-2009, subject to confirmation in the 2006 Spending Review.**

DEVELOPING A PRINCIPLED APPROACH

13   In developing the new proposal for a Local Enterprise Growth Initiative (LEGI), the Government is committed to following a principled approach on the basis of past experience, research, and an ongoing dialogue with key stakeholders in local government, regional institutions, and the business community.

14   The proposal for the LEGI is therefore based on a set of six key principles: effective targeting (to ensure people living in deprived areas benefit); effective solutions (to address the fundamental barriers to growth); significant commitment (of resources over the long term); strong local partnerships (with business and the wider community); integration (with broader regeneration efforts); and evaluation and evidence building (to inform continuous improvement and the development of future policy).

A LOCAL ENTERPRISE GROWTH INITIATIVE

15   Following the six key principles, this document consults on proposals for a Local Enterprise Growth Initiative (LEGI) worth £50 million in 2006-2007, rising to £150 million per year by 2008-2009, subject to confirmation in the 2006 Spending Review.

16   The LEGI will provide flexible, devolved investment in our most deprived areas – determined by the Neighbourhood Renewal Fund areas – to support locally developed and owned proposals that pursue new or proven ways of stimulating economic activity and productivity through enterprise development. The national-level aim of the LEGI is:

"To release the productivity and economic potential of our most deprived local areas and their inhabitants through enterprise and investment – thereby boosting local incomes and employment opportunities."

17   This aim is supported by three outcomes:

1.   To increase **total entrepreneurial activity** among the population in deprived local areas.

2.   To support the **sustainable growth** – and reduce the failure rate – of locally-owned business in deprived areas.

3.   To attract appropriate **inward investment and franchising** into deprived areas, making use of local labour resources.

18   These three outcomes reflect the contribution that business start-ups, growth businesses, and inward investors make to both national-level productivity growth and local economic development in deprived areas. To ensure sustainability over the long-term, the LEGI will be focused on the fundamental issues and barriers that hold back enterprise and growth.

19   The LEGI will follow closely the principles of devolution, providing local institutions and communities with the authority and freedom to best determine local needs, options and solutions for enterprise development in deprived areas. Within the three broad outcomes set out above, there will be significant discretion to determine what the local priorities should be and how to tackle them – what indicators to aim for, what actions to pursue, and what local targets are needed.

20   The resources provided by the LEGI will be targeted at in-depth interventions in a determined number of local authority areas with both a need (measured by level of deprivation) and potential (business potential inhibited by market failures). Therefore, local authorities that are designated as Neighbourhood Renewal Fund areas will be eligible for LEGI support. The aim of the LEGI is to make a long-term change, transforming local deprived areas by addressing the market failures that inhibit growth, ensuring the change is sustainable beyond the life of the policy.

21   Individual local authorities that are successful in applying for LEGI support should expect to receive a significant sum of money – anything between £2-10 million depending on the 'critical mass' of resources required in different areas. This level of funding will be available for these authorities for a significant period of time (anything from five to ten years) to support their proposals for enterprise development – illustrating the Government's significant commitment to reviving these local economies over the long-term.

NEXT STEPS

22   The Government welcomes the views of all stakeholders on the questions raised in this consultation document. The closing date for consultation responses is Wednesday 8 June.

STRUCTURE OF THIS DOCUMENT

23   The remainder of this consultation document is divided into six chapters:

- **Chapter 1** briefly sets-out the macroeconomic context for enterprise, summarising the contribution of enterprise to UK productivity growth, and the enterprise gap between the UK and its main economic competitors – driving the Government's overall **enterprise vision**;

- **Chapter 2** discusses **enterprise in deprived areas**, focusing on the opportunities for enterprise, and the contribution of enterprise to local economic development;

- **Chapter 3** sets-out the issues concerned with **tackling the enterprise gap** in deprived areas, focusing on the barriers to enterprise, and an introduction to the Government's approach to tackling this problem;

- **Chapter 4** outlines a set of **key principles** to guide policy on enterprise in deprived areas, resulting from lessons learnt from research, international experience, and from a dialogue with key stakeholders from local government, the regional development agencies, and the business community;

- **Chapter 5** sets-out the key details of the proposal to establish a new **Local Enterprise Growth Initiative**, and asks for views; and

- **Chapter 6** summarises the **key questions for consultation** and provides information on the next steps in the consultation process.

THE ENTERPRISE VISION

"Our starting point is the importance of enterprise to the future of our country. For my mission for Britain – indeed the key to our future economic success and social cohesion – is a country where enterprise is truly open to all, a nation of aspiration and ambition united in encouraging and celebrating innovation and enterprise... Britain is uniquely well placed to become one of the strongest, most successful enterprise centres of the world."

(Rt Hon Gordon Brown MP, Chancellor of the Exchequer, 2004)

SUMMARY

1.1   Enterprise is one of the key drivers of the productivity of the UK economy. Building a strong enterprise culture and environment is vital in closing the productivity gap that exists between the UK and its main competitors.

1.2   The Government's vision is that anybody with the talent, potential and drive to succeed in business should have the opportunity and necessary support to do so, regardless of their background or where they live.

1.3   Therefore, the Government has a key role to play in ensuring the right conditions are in place for enterprise to flourish across the economy, both by building an enterprise friendly environment, and by correcting for specific market failures that create obstacles to successful enterprise.

THE PRODUCTIVITY GAP

1.4   An economy's output depends on two things: how many people are working; and how much they produce – that is how productive they are.[1] While UK employment has performed well over recent years, UK productivity has not fared as well. In particular, there has been a significant and long-standing productivity gap between the UK and some of its key economic competitors – including the US, France and Germany – as Chart 1.1 below shows.

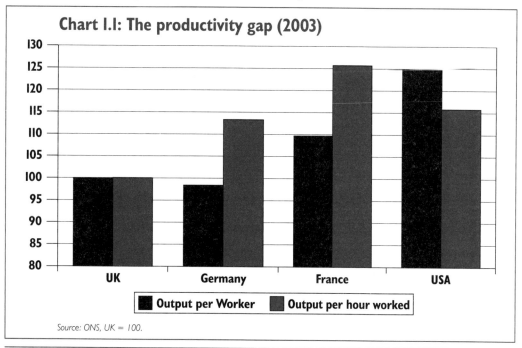

Chart 1.1: The productivity gap (2003)

Source: ONS, UK = 100.

---

[1] For a full exposition of this see: *Trend Growth: Prospects and Implications for policy*, HM Treasury (1999).

I.5   The Government has a clear strategy to narrow the productivity gap over the longer-term, comprising two elements: the first is the macroeconomic framework, which has delivered the longest sustained period of stable economic growth for 200 years, kept interest rates at their lowest level for over 30 years, and achieved the longest period of low and stable inflation since the 1960s; the second is a series of microeconomic reforms based around the five key drivers of productivity:

- competition;

- **enterprise**;

- science and innovation (R&D);

- skills (human capital); and

- investment (physical capital).

I.6   This consultation paper addresses part of the Government's strategy to raise levels of enterprise in England – with a particular focus on raising levels of enterprise in deprived areas – as part of the wider drive to develop local economies and drive productivity growth.

ENTERPRISE AND PRODUCTIVITY

I.7   Entrepreneurship can be defined as the mindset and process by which an individual or group identifies and successfully exploits a new idea or opportunity. It requires creativity, ambition, independence, and the willingness to bear the inevitable risks involved. This consultation paper focuses on two particular forms of enterprise: the creation of new businesses; and enterprising behaviour within existing small and medium-sized firms. In addition, deprived areas can often benefit from appropriate inward investment – the location of existing firms within the deprived area to drive local productivity and economic growth.

I.8   Key to understanding enterprise in the present day is a brief examination of the dynamics of small business in the UK economy over the last 100 years.

Box 1.1: Enterprise in the twentieth century

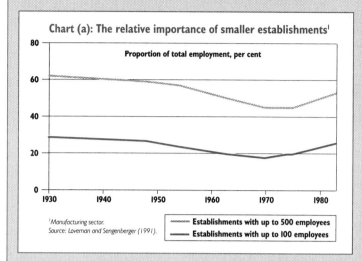

Chart (a): The relative importance of smaller establishments[1]

Proportion of total employment, per cent

[1] Manufacturing sector.
Source: Loveman and Sengenberger (1991).

······· Establishments with up to 500 employees
——— Establishments with up to 100 employees

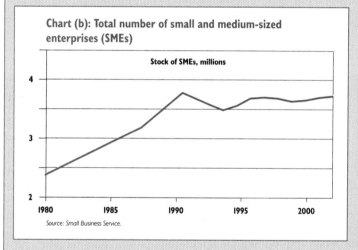

Chart (b): Total number of small and medium-sized enterprises (SMEs)

Stock of SMEs, millions

Source: Small Business Service.

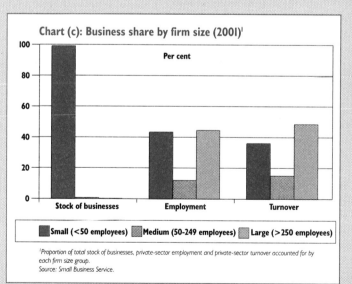

Chart (c): Business share by firm size (2001)[1]

Per cent

Stock of businesses   Employment   Turnover

■ Small (<50 employees)   ▨ Medium (50-249 employees)   ▨ Large (>250 employees)

[1] Proportion of total stock of businesses, private-sector employment and private-sector turnover accounted for by each firm size group.
Source: Small Business Service.

During much of the twentieth century, production in the UK and across the industrialised world became increasingly concentrated in large-scale plants and organisations – exploiting economies of scale from mass production. Small businesses share of total employment fell progressively and was considered to be in a state of long-term decline.

However, since the 1970s – as a result of increasing globalisation of economic activity and the shift within the UK from a manufacturing to a service-based economy – there has been a significant resurgence in small business activity. Small to medium-sized enterprises (SMEs) became the principal engine of employment growth in the 1970s and,[2] since 1980, the total stock of SMEs has increased from around 2.5 million to 4 million today.[3]

During the late 1990s, SMEs accounted for over 50 per cent of all job creation in expanding firms. New firms established during the period had provided 2.3 million new jobs by 1999 – over 85 per cent of which were in SMEs.[4]

SMEs today make a substantial contribution to the UK economy, with more than 99 per cent of all firms employing fewer than 50 staff (and many are sole traders). Collectively, SMEs account for over 55 per cent of private-sector employment, and over 50 per cent of private-sector turnover.

[2] Loveman and Sengenberger (1991).
[3] HM Treasury (2002).
[4] Dale Morgan (2001).

Enterprise and productivity

1.9 Among major industrialised economies, levels of entrepreneurship are positively correlated with both the level of per capita Gross Domestic Product (GDP) and the rate of GDP growth.[2] This is consistent with the view that an enterprising small business sector contributes to economic performance. As Figure 1.1 shows this contribution may take a number of forms.

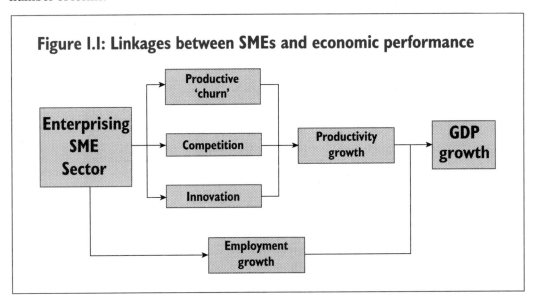

Figure 1.1: Linkages between SMEs and economic performance

1.10 First, enterprise is a key driver of productivity growth in its own right. The creation and growth of new firms, and the implementation of novel ideas within existing businesses, contribute to the beneficial process of **productive 'churn'**, by which market share is transferred through market forces from lower-productivity plants and firms to their more productive counterparts. This raises productivity at an aggregate level.

1.11 Second, enterprise interacts with other drivers of productivity growth. Enterprise is an important driver of **competition**: in attempting to raise their own market share, firms of all sizes provide a continual incentive for their competitors to invest, innovate, and seek efficiency and quality improvements. Enterprising SMEs also play a key role in the process of **innovation**, experimenting with new ideas and putting them into practice. SMEs play an important role in 'innovation networks', for example, by providing specialist equipment and services to boost the innovative potential of larger firms.

THE ENTERPRISE CHALLENGE

1.12 Despite the rapid growth of the SME sector since the 1970s, rates of entrepreneurial activity in the UK remain only moderate by international standards.[3] It is estimated that around 5.5 per cent of working age adults are engaged either in starting a new business or in running a young firm in the UK.[4] This figure is close to the European average, but is barely over half the US level. Moreover, the UK appears to lag behind the US in terms of high-growth start-ups – new firms in the US typically expand more rapidly than those in Europe.[5]

---

[2] OECD (2001), Audretsch and Thurik (2001).

[3] Department of Trade and Industry (2002).

[4] Reynolds *et al* (2002).

[5] Scarpetta *et al* (2002).

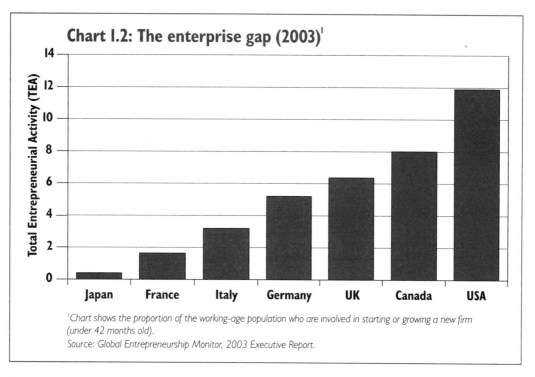

Chart 1.2: The enterprise gap (2003)[1]

Total Entrepreneurial Activity (TEA)

Japan France Italy Germany UK Canada USA

[1]Chart shows the proportion of the working-age population who are involved in starting or growing a new firm (under 42 months old).
Source: Global Entrepreneurship Monitor, 2003 Executive Report.

1.13 To ensure the potential economic and social benefits of enterprise are exploited as fully as possible, it is vital that the opportunity to participate in enterprise should be open to anybody with the talent and potential to do so, and that the right conditions should be in place for individuals to start and grow successful businesses.

1.14 There is some evidence of improvements in the enterprise environment in the UK. The OECD has rated the UK as having the lowest barriers to entrepreneurship of any major economy. Similarly, the World Bank's study *Doing Business in 2005* places the UK top in the European Union, and seventh in the top twenty economies in the world, with the best business conditions – and also ranks the UK fifth in terms of the cost of starting a business, less costly than both France and Germany.

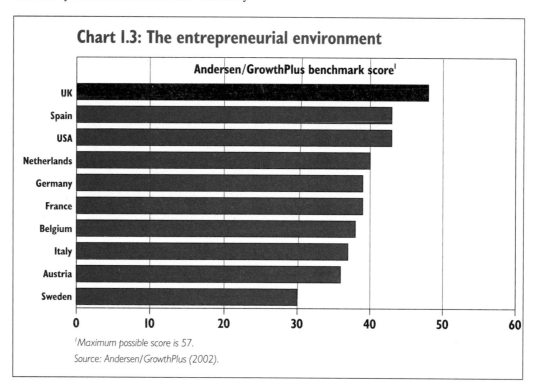

Chart 1.3: The entrepreneurial environment

Andersen/GrowthPlus benchmark score[1]

UK
Spain
USA
Netherlands
Germany
France
Belgium
Italy
Austria
Sweden

0 10 20 30 40 50 60

[1]Maximum possible score is 57.
Source: Andersen/GrowthPlus (2002).

THE GOVERNMENT'S ENTERPRISE VISION

1.15   The Government's enterprise vision is that anybody with the talent, potential and drive to succeed in business should have the opportunity and the necessary support to do so, regardless of their background or where they live.

1.16   Entrepreneurs and small business owners themselves are the most important agents in delivering this vision. The Government – both central and local – has an important role to play in creating a fertile business environment, addressing market failures and ensuring that, where it comes into contact with future entrepreneurs and existing businesses, it helps rather than hinders them. This role is all the more important in deprived areas, where barriers to enterprise are often more acute and more persistent than elsewhere.

1.17   Therefore, Government has a key role to play in ensuring that the right conditions are in place for enterprise to flourish across the economy. There are two key strands to Government's strategy in this area:

- to build an **enterprise friendly environment.** It is vital that talented individuals should consider running their own business to be a valuable and rewarding career option, that the right conditions are in place for businesses to thrive and prosper, and that government regulations are fair and proportionate; and

- to correct for specific **market failures** that create obstacles to successful enterprise. Relative to larger firms, SMEs face particular barriers to accessing finance, lack awareness of the availability and potential advantages of external business advice, and face difficulties appropriating the full benefits of both training, and research and development (R&D).

1.18   The Government's approach in each of these two areas is set-out in detail in the HM Treasury and Small Business Service publication *Enterprise Britain: A Modern Approach to Meeting the Enterprise Challenge* (2002).[6]

---

[6] HM Treasury/Small Business Service (2002).

2 ENTERPRISE IN DEPRIVED AREAS

"We recognise that the barriers to enterprise are greater in poor communities and that many businesses in our least well off areas face special problems in obtaining access to support, advice and finance. Our objective is that no-one is left out on the margins, no-one excluded from the mainstream of economic prosperity. And this is the time - when economic growth is strengthening - to do more to bring prosperity to those places and people the economy has too often and for too long forgotten."

(Rt Hon Gordon Brown MP, Chancellor of the Exchequer, 2003)

SUMMARY

2.1 At the local level, all local authorities have a key role to play in developing the economies of local areas – working with their regional development agencies (RDAs) – to pursue their well-being power to promote the economic vitality of localities, as provided for in the Local Government Act 2000.

2.2 In particular, enterprise provides local authorities with a powerful means of pursuing sustainable economic development in deprived areas. Enterprise can contribute to the economic development of deprived areas through:

- local productivity growth;
- employment and income growth;
- improved local service provision;
- creating multiplier effects and building supply chains;
- increasing the local tax base;
- improving the physical environment; and
- investing in the community and building social capital.

2.3 Deprived areas can also present competitive advantages and opportunities for enterprise that are not always taken advantage of – often presenting a strategic location close to transport and communication links; an untapped market demand; possibilities for clustering and multiplier effects; a pool of under-utilised labour; and often a significant commitment of public resources.

LOCAL ECONOMIC DEVELOPMENT

2.4 A central plank of the Government's economic philosophy is that it is not possible to run a successful economic policy without decentralisation and devolution to local and regional levels. This makes it imperative that local authorities and other local and regional bodies have a clear economic development role, which they must have the capacity and leadership, the flexibility and the policy levers to carry-out. Since 1997, the Government has strengthened the role and influence of the regions and local areas of England. This devolved approach to economic policy approach rests on two key principles:

1. it aims to strengthen the long-term building blocks of growth, innovation, skills and the development of enterprise by exploiting the indigenous strengths of each region, city and locality.

2. it is bottom-up and not top-down, with national government enabling powerful regional and local initiatives to work by providing the necessary flexibility and resources.

The economic development role of local authorities

2.5 The large disparities between local areas in terms of both inputs and outputs of economic development mean that it is essential that economic development policy is implemented at the local level. Evidence supports this in principle as the individual characteristics of places are very different and it is only possible to create effective policies and partnerships with considerable local knowledge. History, culture and local outlook, for example, all play a role in explaining what the challenges are for a local economy and what the capacity is to address them.

2.6 To encourage more local authorities to see economic development as a crucial part of their mission as community leaders, central and local government agreed on the need to *"promote the economic vitality of localities"* as one of the seven shared priorities from the 2002 Spending Review. Local authorities can and must have a central role in shaping regional economic strategies, and in leading and developing partnerships to take forward these agreed strategies. However, their role goes much wider and is crucially concerned with economic development as an important part of improving the well-being of their area.

2.7 Looking at local authorities that place economic development at the centre of their mission, it is possible to see what can be achieved.

Box 2.1: Economic development in Blackburn with Darwen

Blackburn with Darwen Borough Council has economic development at the heart of its local strategy. This focus has allowed the Council to develop innovative approaches such as providing incubator space for small firms in the borough, allowing new businesses access to meeting and conference space, and business support for free. Further, the digital development unit there, again funded by the Council, provides support in how best to use technology to around 200 business a year. In developing the local economy, Blackburn with Darwen have pursued a true partnership approach.

The Blackburn with Darwen Partnership was established in 1988. It actively involves over 250 companies as well as voluntary and community groups, and runs a series of projects to encourage economic growth in the area. For instance, it supports small, growing businesses, provides links between employers and the community and links all the schools in the borough to private companies. The partnership also works closely with the Council in working to attract new resources to the area, create networks between the public, private and voluntary sectors, and ensuring that the private and public sectors work closely on regeneration projects.

As a result of these efforts and initiatives the number of business start-ups within the area is rising by about 50 per year.

2.8   Economic development of deprived areas is a vitally important part of broader regeneration efforts – such as through the National Strategy for Neighbourhood Renewal.

Box 2.2: National Strategy for Neighbourhood Renewal[1]

The Government published its National Strategy for Neighbourhood Renewal in January 2001. The aim of the strategy is to narrow the gap between outcomes in deprived areas and the rest of the country. It builds on the work of 18 Policy Action Teams, involving hundreds of people inside and outside Government, and thousands of people across the country through consultation.

The Action Plan set out a new approach to renewing poor neighbourhoods. This approach is different for four reasons.

- First, the true scale of the problem is being addressed - not the tens but the hundreds of severely deprived neighbourhoods.

- Second, the focus is not just on housing and the physical fabric of neighbourhoods, but the fundamental problems of worklessness, crime and poor public services - poor schools, too few General Practitioners, and policing.

- Third, the strategy harnesses the hundreds of billions of pounds spent by the key Government departments, rather than relying on one-off regeneration spending.

- Fourth, the strategy puts in place new ideas including Neighbourhood Management and Local Strategic Partnerships for empowering residents and getting public, private and voluntary organisations to work in partnership.

Building on the progress made to date, the Spending Review 2004 announced continued support for Neighbourhood Renewal of £525 million a year through to 2007-2008, and a refined Public Service Agreement to narrow the gap in key outcomes between the most deprived areas and the rest of the country.[2]

[1] Office of the Deputy Prime Minister (2001).
[2] HM Treasury (2004).

Building partnerships   2.9   Though local authorities have a crucial, and often central, role in delivering economic development and improved prosperity in their area, as the Blackburn with Darwen example illustrated, it is impossible to achieve success on their own. Working closely with business groups and individual businesses is particularly important. It is crucial that the public and private sectors engage constructively around shared objectives to improve local economic performance. This requires both local authorities and businesses to understand each other's approach and needs, and to work flexibly to meet their aims.

2.10   Therefore, an enterprise development plan is not just about a local authority allocating its own funding, but is a much wider community leadership role. It is important to recognise that the amount of money spent by the regional development agencies (RDAs) and local authorities on economic development specifically is small in comparison to total spending in a local area on services that will impact on economic vitality, such as schools and local learning and skills councils. This further emphasises the need for local authorities to work in partnership in delivering positive economic outcomes and is the rationale behind community strategies.

Increasing 2.11   The Government believes that devolving decision making from the centre to regional
devolution and local levels is critical to success in improving service delivery and economic
development.

2.12   The Government has significantly increased the freedoms and flexibilities of regional
development agencies, devolving new responsibilities for Business Link and other areas,
within a strengthened performance management framework.

2.13   In the Local Government Act 2000, local authorities were also given wide-sweeping
powers to promote the economic, social and environmental well-being of their area. This
grants local authorities considerable freedom to meet the goals for their area that they agree
with partners as part of the local community strategy.

2.14   Taking this agenda further, the first round of Local Area Agreements, providing
greater financial flexibilities to local areas to better match resources with local priorities, and
enabling closer partnership working, will shortly commence. A further 40 will be negotiated
for commencement in April 2006. More information on Local Area Agreements is provided in
Chapter 5.

2.15   These freedoms and flexibilities help to provide an environment in which local
authorities can act under the well-being power to improve local prosperity. Central to the
actions local authorities take to develop their local economies should be the effective
development of enterprise and business activity.

ENTERPRISE AND ECONOMIC DEVELOPMENT

2.16   The contribution of enterprise to economic development can take a number of
forms: local productivity growth; employment and income growth; increases in local tax
revenue; improved service provision; multiplier effects, supply chains and sub-contracting;
building social capital; improving the physical environment; and community investment and
involvment.

Local productivity growth

2.17   As discussed in Chapter 1, enterprise is a key driver of productivity growth at the
national level. Enterprise in deprived areas will also raise the productivity of the local
economy – with new firms driving product market competition and generating innovations
in technology and organisation – local enterprise is therefore fundamental to sustainable
growth in deprived areas.

Employment and income growth

2.18   In the short-run, employment benefits from new business start-ups are felt by owner-
managers and employees, and will then spread to the wider local community as the business
grows and demand for labour increases. In particular, the self-employed have been shown to
be strongly attached to place – reflecting the personal services orientation of many self-
employed businesses - thereby retaining the employment benefits in the local area.[1] Many
new business start-ups continue to locate and inject money into the deprived local area by
expanding and selling to wider markets over time.

---

[1] Blanchflower (1998) in OECD (2003).

2.19   In particular, franchised businesses that locate in deprived areas can make use of local labour and help generate wealth among the local inhabitants.

Increases in local tax revenue

2.20   New businesses, growth of existing businesses, or inward investment from relocation of businesses into deprived areas can stimulate and grow the local tax base – through business rates – that can be reinvested in the community, public services and in building an environment more conducive to business and enterprise. The Government has recognised the mutually beneficial and reinforcing relationship between local tax and business through the Local Authority Business Growth Incentives (LABGI) scheme, providing local authorities with the incentive to promote business growth and enterprise development.

Box 2.3: Local Authority Business Growth Incentives (LABGI)

At the local level there is currently a mismatch between the costs of economic development and the benefits that accrue from it. Economic development imposes practical costs on local authorities, for the services that they provide to support growth.

In contrast, the benefits of economic growth typically accrue either to individuals, through greater and better employment opportunities or, in tax terms, at the national level. This suggests that while costs of economic development accrue at the local authority level, the benefits accrue at a wider level.

The LABGI scheme is designed to help address this issue. Currently, all business rate revenues are collected by local authorities and passed into a central pool. These revenues are then redistributed on a per capita basis. From 2005 the LABGI scheme will allow local authorities to individually retain some of the business rate revenues that are associated with growing the business rate tax base at the local level.

As such, it should create positive financial incentives for local authorities to work with business, regional development agencies, Learning and Skills Councils and other key local and regional stakeholders to maximise local economic growth.

The Government has conducted two full consultations and an administrative dry-run involving 40 volunteer local authorities over the last two years. The final scheme, begining in April, will directly reflect the Government's consultative approach to its development.

Improved service provision

2.21   Key to the successful economic development of deprived areas is the retention of money flows within the local area. Increased service provision by locally-owned businesses – such as retail provision – is one way of ensuring money flows benefit the local area and do not 'leak' into neighbouring areas. For example, shopper surveys carried-out by Experian on behalf of the Office of the Deputy Prime Minister show that the majority of spend from Salford residents is diverted to Manchester City Centre, whereas spend to local centres within the council boundary accounts for less than 20 per cent of the total resident spend.[2]

2.22   A greater level of local service provision also directly benefits local inhabitants who benefit from access to vital services. A survey of 20 poor localities in the UK found that none had a supermarket or similar shops, and only five had a chemist or launderette.[3] In particular, the provision of local services is beneficial for those without access to suitable modes of transport – and is particularly important in some rural and suburban areas.

---

[2] Business in the Community (2005).
[3] Cabinet Office (1998) in OECD (2003).

2.23   Sometimes, the development of socially enterprising businesses can provide vital services that the state or market cannot or will not provide – and often can compete on equal terms with the private (i.e. profit-distributing) and state sectors.[4] Social enterprises – part of the broader third sector – can also contribute to enterprise development, through provision of finance and investment opportunities to other small businesses.

Box 2.4: The social entrepreneurs of Blaengwnfi[1]

An ex-mining village of 2000 people, in economic decline, was faced with the closure of its only shop for 12 miles. The concerned senior citizen's group enlisted the help of the local business support provider (now a Business Link), obtained a bank loan and raised the deposit money for the building from selling shares in the village.

After a year of successful trading they obtained finance from the council to renovate the shop and convert the rest of the building into retail units. By retaining money flows within the local area and supporting local enterprise, the neighbourhood benefited from a stronger economy.

In ten years the co-operative paid-off the shop mortgage and now feeds its profits back into new community projects. The retail units house several businesses, some of which have since moved out into their own premises as they have grown. Future plans include starting a new social enterprise – a leisure and tourism cooperative.

[1] HM Treasury (1999).

Multiplier effect, supply chains and sub-contracting

2.24   Enterprise development in deprived local areas also creates demand for other businesses – from either the service sector (e.g. business services) or from manufacturing and wholesaling (e.g. food produce). As well as helping to grow local supply chains, businesses may also grow to the extent that they enter into sub-contracting relationships with other local businesses. This knock-on effect onto other businesses, and the subsequent generation of further economic activity is often known as the multiplier effect. The multiplier effect may be more prominent for less specialist products and services who may be more likely to source locally and have more local customers.[5]

Building social capital

2.25   Social capital can be defined as the development of active social networks and trust between and within communities. Social capital development is important to enterprise development as social networks can provide links between existing entrepreneurs and aspiring entrepreneurs, and also between existing businesses – allowing collaborative activities including sharing of equipment, ideas and information, referrals, and joint projects.[6] Social capital generated through enterprise development can also improve the levels of community cohesion and trust that is so important in deprived areas.

---

[4] See *Exploring the Role of the Third Sector in Public Service Delivery and Reform*, HM Treasury (2005) for further information.
[5] Small Business Service (2002).
[6] *Ibid.*

Improving the physical environment

2.26   Sometimes, the creation of new businesses in deprived areas can help drive a physical renewal. The reclamation of brownfield land and derelict buildings in particular in distressed urban areas can lead to a positive cycle of improvement, attracting other businesses and residents, and potentially further public investment to develop the local physical environment.

Box 2.5: Hastings Borough Council and business working together to improve the physical environment

Working together, businesses and the Council have achieved a dramatic turnaround in the appearance and vitality of the Hastings town centre and seafront. The transformation started with the £40 million Priory Meadow shopping centre, developed in 1997 by Boots plc. This established 50 new units, which were rapidly filled by major national chains, creating over 400 new jobs in one of the UK's 10 per cent most deprived wards.

However, the new development threatened to pull businesses and customers away from traditional shopping streets. Meanwhile, once attractive seafront buildings were suffering from long-term under-maintenance. The Council initiated a programme of environmental improvements and incentives to renovate facades and refurbish interiors. Retailers, hoteliers and residential landlords have responded by investing over £10 million in properties and staff. The key outcomes have been declining vacancy rates, from 17 per cent to 5 per cent, in the old core retail area, and a further 150 new jobs. There has also been a qualitative shift towards mainly independently run new shops, bars and restaurants.

The approach has been extended into St Leonards, while the RDA-backed Sea Space task force for Hastings and Bexhill brings more pump-priming investment. With a new landmark Media Centre drawing small creative businesses into the area, Hastings has the beginnings of a café culture. Hotels have been upgraded, the town again has a seafront it can take pride in, and Hastings as a whole is more attractive to visitors and inward investors.

Community investment and involvement

2.27   Local businesses and entrepreneurs often invest extra resources in their local communities – from supporting and participating in local community groups, providing encouragement and guidance to other members of the community and helping other local businesses.[7] Larger businesses often have corporate social responsibility programmes, but smaller businesses also engage in significant community activities – contributing to the local social and community fabric above and beyond their business activities. The Office of the Deputy Prime Minister's Private Sector Panel on neighbourhood renewal developed a menu of such opportunities, and the Business Broker pilot programme demonstrated a threefold increase in business engagement in the pilot areas.

---

[7] Small Business Service (2002).

Box 2.6: Inner City 100 and community involvement[1]

The Inner City 100 (IC 100) was launched in 2001 focusing on enterprise as a key driver of regeneration. The IC 100 celebrated the entrepreneurial drive, innovation and competitiveness of fast-growing inner-city businesses and has worked to shatter perceptions of the UK's inner cities as no go areas for enterprise with positive role models. The IC 100 also highlighted and encouraged the contributions that inner city businesses make to their local economies and communities.

The 2004 IC 100 data showed that for these 100 firms:

- financial and non-financial contributions to their local communities are estimated at £7 million;

- 79 per cent were directly involved in their local communities and 90 per cent of those in more than one activity;

- over one quarter were engaged in mentoring other entrepreneurs, which helps to address the significant problem of a lack of enterprising role models in deprived areas; and

- in terms of the benefits that this community involvement delivers to them more than half the firms said it built morale within the company and enhanced the company profile; 41 per cent believe engagement in the community helps with networking; and 33 per cent said it helps with recruitment.

[1] New Economics Foundation (2004).

Limitations and pitfalls

2.28 However, enterprise and economic development is not a simple or easy task. The benefits that can be derived from enterprise in particular localities need to be considered on a case-by-case basis. In particular, local plans for enterprise development need to consider the possible pitfalls inherent in promoting a business-led economic development programme, and design local strategies to minimise such negative externalities.

Displacement **2.29** Displacement occurs when competition from new firms causes a loss of output or employment in existing enterprises.[8] New business start-ups in deprived areas tend to be in similar sectors of the economy – with low barriers to entry and lower skill or capital requirements – thereby exacerbating the displacement effect.

2.30 However, it must be noted that displacement can sometimes have a positive impact, if more efficient and innovative firms replace others – raising local productivity through productive churn – or if it generates new employment opportunities for local residents.

Need for **2.31** Enterprise development alone cannot successfully develop local economies and **integration** regenerate local communities, but must take place as part of a wider sustainable community strategy and set of interventions on, for example, health, education, crime and housing. Local areas therefore need to develop – as part of the local sustainable community strategy – a comprehensive and integrated strategy that combines efforts on enterprise development with wider efforts on neighbourhood renewal. The introduction of Local Area Agreements provides a new way of ensuring funding supports this integrated approach.

---

[8] OECD (2003).

Employment leakage   **2.32**   The relationship between the employment opportunities and occupational structure presented by new businesses or inward investors and the local labour supply is vitally important in internalising the benefits to the local areas. If there is a mismatch between the local labour supply and the employment opportunities presented (for example, a high-technology firm locates in a deprived area with a need for very specific skills set from its employees) there is a high probability that there will be inward migration of labour from other areas – leaving the local unemployment rate largely unchanged. Local plans for enterprise development will need to understand the characteristics of the local labour supply if they are to effectively handle issues of inward labour migration.

Quality of employment   **2.33**   Central to effective enterprise development strategies is the need to consider the quality of employment created – be that self-employment or employment in a new business venture. For example, while the self-employed often have higher levels of job satisfaction than employees,[9] they are also exposed to lower and more volatile earnings, long working hours, and fewer benefit entitlements.[10]

Targeting the vulnerable   **2.34**   Those individuals in deprived areas that possess greater skills, finance and social assets will undoubtedly benefit greatly from enterprise development strategies. Indeed, entrepreneurship in deprived areas may in fact demand greater aptitude from aspiring entrepreneurs than in other contexts.[11] However, those tasked with enterprise development in deprived areas will need to also ensure they provide sufficient support and attention to the most vulnerable groups in these areas.

Time lags   **2.35**   In developing proposals for local enterprise development it is important to understand that the benefits – or positive externalities – that arise from entrepreneurial activity in deprived areas will take time to become apparent. Most new business start-ups will require consolidation of activity and an increase in turnover over the initial few years before they are able to expand employment opportunities to the wider community. As the OECD have noted:

"The relatively long gestation periods involved in business creation and development suggest that entrepreneurship strategies should be policy constants [over the medium to long-term], rather than responses to short-term employment crises."

(OECD, 2003)

OPPORTUNITIES FOR ENTERPRISE

2.36   Enterprise clearly has a central role to play in developing the local economies of deprived areas. However, it is also important to make clear that deprived areas provide market opportunities and competitive advantages that can create a business case for potential inward investors or aspiring entrepreneurs. Rather than seeing deprived areas as 'no go' areas for business and enterprise, inward investors and aspiring entrepreneurs should recognise the potential and opportunities that deprived areas can offer. Local authorities in particular should invest in identifying the potential competitive advantages such areas offer – such as those identified by Michael Porter (1995), including strategic location, local market demand, and clustering and supply chains etc.

---

[9] Blanchflower (1998) in OECD (2003).

[10] OECD (2003).

[11] *Ibid.*

Strategic location

2.37   Deprived areas can provide a strategic location for new business or inward investors, offering many advantages such as close access to transport, communication, and leisure facilities. Deprived areas may be close to inner city retail areas, providing supply-chain opportunities, and may also offer the prospect of good quality back office, support, and logistics functions. For example, many of the logistics of the new economy, such as just-in-time delivery and instant service, often play to the strengths of deprived inner-city areas.

Local market demand

2.38   Deprived communities can also sometimes offer an untapped market demand from local residents who are poorly served in terms of access to vital goods and services. As such, deprived areas can provide the opportunity for early entrants to gain a competitive advantage in establishing and building market share.

Box 2.7: Investment in Under-served Markets Project – Harlem

The Under-served Markets Project was launched by the Office of the Deputy Prime Minister in 2003, building on the practical experience of the business-led regeneration of Harlem, New York. Harlem was previously a neighbourhood marked by poverty, high crime and dilapidated buildings, but has undergone a radical shift from a 'no go' area to a thriving economic community.

Collaborations between local stakeholders and the business community have led to successful inward investments. In 1997, a new bank was opened followed, in 1999, by the development of a shopping centre attracting a major supermarket chain and creating 210 permanent jobs. In 2000, a shopping retail complex was opened attracting major national retailers, sustaining existing gains. A major office, hotel and retail development are due to open in 2006 followed by a further plaza in 2007.

The success of business led regeneration in Harlem was underpinned by:

- a strong partnership between local stakeholders and the business community;
- communicating business opportunities, as initial business perceptions of the area were of households with no middle class presence, no buying power, and a significant crime problem. In reality: 20 per cent of households have an annual income of $50,000 or more; and rather than a lack of customers, the problem was that 70 per cent of residents shopped outside the area due to low levels of service provision within the area; and crime around underground stations in Harlem was shown to be no greater than Times Square and Wall Street; and
- a strong entrepreneurial immigrant population meant that measures of economic activity were often not captured by traditional statistics.

2.39   Investing in an under-served market also has the potential to build a strong relationship between both the business and the community. Businesses have the opportunity to build a strong brand image with the local community as the area becomes more prosperous.

Clustering and supply chains

2.40   The Government's 1998 Competitiveness White Paper *Our Competitive Future: Building the Knowledge Driven Economy* highlighted that business development is often strongest when firms cluster together – creating a critical mass of growth, collaboration, competition and opportunities for investment and knowledge sharing and the development of effective supply chains.[12]

2.41   Deprived areas can offer opportunities for local agglomeration and the multiplier effects that result from this. Evidence – including the Harlem example above – has shown that when one business locates in an area, it can become an 'anchor' institution and attract other firms in a cluster that can either benefit from the same market or from the supply chains created by that firm.

Human resources

2.42   Deprived areas can sometimes offer a pool of under-utilised human resources that can provide the necessary employment basis for some businesses and inward investors. While there can be difficulties associated with both the levels of skills and transition from benefits to business, there is significant untapped labour potential in some deprived areas that – with the help of integrated local employment and enterprise development strategies – could be brought back into the active labour force.

Public investment

2.43   Finally, the Government has committed significant resources in pursuit of the objective of regenerating deprived areas. This public investment can provide much needed support to develop the business environment in deprived areas. Furthermore, the long-term nature of this investment provides a degree of certainty to aspiring entrepreneurs and inward investors of the continued Government commitment to support, improve and regenerate the local area.

---

[12] Cited in *Trends Business Research* for Department of Trade and Industry (2001).

3 TACKLING THE ENTERPRISE GAP

"we share a common purpose - a common agenda. To make sure that we maximise potential and abilities, so that we can spread the growth to every community, every area and every region."

(Rt Hon John Prescott MP, Deputy Prime Minister, 2003)

SUMMARY

3.1 Levels of enterprise in deprived areas are significantly and persistently lower than in more affluent areas. Fewer businesses start-up in deprived areas and have a higher failure rate than elsewhere.

3.2 Government should therefore intervene for two reasons:

1. **Efficiency:** local economies in deprived areas suffer from market failures that mean they are less efficient and productive than they could be.

2. **Equity:** concentrations of deprivation raise deep equity concerns in terms of sub-optimal outcomes for local people – from access to jobs, to health, and crime.

3.3 While deprived areas often present competitive advantages and opportunities, they can also present significant barriers that are either more acute or more persistent than in more affluent areas. Barriers in deprived areas relate to: the ability of the entrepreneur or small business to access suitable finance and business support services; the lack of experience, skills or training of potential employees; a weak enterprise culture; a greater incidence of institutional or administrative barriers; and/or a poor business environment.

3.4 Therefore, Government proposes three 'pillars' of support for enterprise in deprived areas:

1. **National:** tackling certain key enterprise development issues at the national level through a strengthened Enterprise Areas package, where either economies of scale are required, or where issues are common across many areas.

2. **Regional:** devolving to the regional level new responsibilities for the delivery of Business Link and the Phoenix Fund, to enable an integrated approach to business support.

3. **Local:** building on support through the Neighbourhood Renewal Strategy, providing significant commitment to support locally appropriate plans for enterprise development through a Local Enterprise Growth Initiative worth £50 million in 2006-2007, rising to £150 million per year by 2008-2009 subject to confirmation in the 2006 Spending Review.

ENTERPRISE GAP

Regional **3.5**   There are significant disparities in levels of enterprise within the UK. At a regional
disparities level there is a wide variation in both business start-up rates and business density – in the
North East, only 23 businesses per 10,000 residents registered for VAT in 2003, compared with
the UK average of 40. Over time, differences in business creation rates contribute to a marked
disparity in the total stock of businesses – for example in 2003 there were 219 VAT registered
businesses for every 10,000 residents in the North East, compared with a UK average of 378.[1,2]

Table 3.1: Start-up rates and business stock levels by region (2003)

	Start-ups per 10,000 resident adults[1]	Start-ups as a proportion of total business stock[2] (per cent)	Total business stock per 10,000 resident adults[3]
United Kingdom	40	11	378
North East	23	11	219
North West	35	11	314
Yorkshire and the Humber	34	11	320
East Midlands	37	10	361
West Midlands	37	10	357
East of England	42	10	417
London	62	13	481
South East	47	11	439
South West	40	10	416
England	42	11	385
Wales	29	9	337
Scotland	29	9	307
Northern Ireland	29	7	444

[1] VAT registrations during 2003 per 10,000 resident adults at mid-2003.

[2] VAT registrations during 2003 as a proportion of the stock of VAT-registered businesses at the start of 2003.

[3] Stock of VAT-registered businesses at the start of 2003 per 10,000 resident adults at mid-2004.

Source: Small Business Service (2004).

3.6   Promoting enterprise in deprived areas is an important part of the Government's
strategy to reduce regional economic disparities, alongside employment and skills. In 2002
the Government introduced an objective, updated in 2004, to *make sustainable
improvements in the economic performance of all English regions by 2008, and over the long-
term reduce the persistent gap in growth rates between the English regions, demonstrating
progress by 2006.* Low levels of enterprise are a significant cause of poor economic
performance in certain regions.

[1] Differences in economic performance between UK regions are discussed in HM Treasury: *Productivity in the UK: 3 – the
regional dimension* (2001).

[2] To an extent, VAT registration data may exaggerate the difference in levels of economic activity, as they do not capture
businesses that lie below the VAT turnover threshold. Such businesses may form a higher proportion of businesses in
deprived areas. However, differences also show up in self-employment rates, which are substantially below the UK
average in disadvantaged communities. See Kempson and Mackinnon (2002).

Box 3.1: The Northern Way Growth Strategy

The three northern regional development agencies (RDAs), along with other regional partners, published *The Northern Way: First Growth Strategy Report* in September 2004.[1] This sets out an ambitious strategy to establish the North of England as an area of exceptional opportunity with a world-class economy and a superb quality of life.

The Growth Strategy identified low levels of entrepreneurship as one of the key barriers to higher growth in the North. It set itself the aim to increase the rate of new business start-ups from 30 per 10,000 people to 33 per 10,000 people by 2008.

In January, the Northern Way published a progress report, detailing its plans to build a more entrepreneurial North. Two main themes are:

* **Northern Enterprise in Education Programme**: building on the national strategy for Enterprise in Education, the aim is to provide a continuum of enterprise activity from primary schools to graduate level.

* **Northern Enterprise Initiative**: includes a pan-northern Women in Enterprise programme, measures to attract entrepreneurs and talented individuals to the north, and a Northern Leadership Academy.

Government has welcomed the Northern Way proposals, and in September agreed to match the RDA contribution to create a £100 million Northern Way Growth Fund to help translate the strategy into practical action. The 2004 Spending Review supported this approach by devolving more freedom, flexibilities, and funding to support economic growth in the North. In the 2004 Pre-Budget Report, the government also announced a number of specific measures that responded to Northern Way proposals.

---

[1] *Moving forward: The Northern Way: First Growth Strategy Report*, The Northern Way Steering Group (2004).

Deprivation and enterprise

3.7   However, intra-regional disparities are as significant as the inter-regional disparities. Excluding London, in 2003 the 20 most deprived local authority districts in England had 28 business start-ups per 10,000 residents, compared with 58 in the 20 least deprived districts. A study by the Bank of England concluded that "the negative relationship between deprivation and entrepreneurial activity appears to be clear-cut in the case of the 50 most deprived local authorities" and more generally, high levels of local deprivation appear to be associated with low business-formation rates as Chart 3.1 illustrates.[4]

---

[3] HM Treasury/ODPM (2003).
[4] Bank of England (2000).

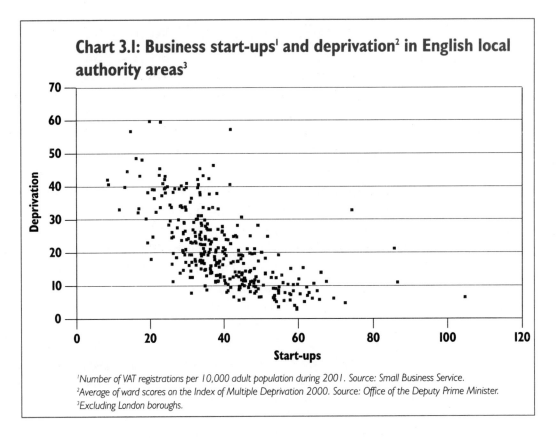

Chart 3.1: Business start-ups[1] and deprivation[2] in English local authority areas[3]

[1] Number of VAT registrations per 10,000 adult population during 2001. Source: Small Business Service.
[2] Average of ward scores on the Index of Multiple Deprivation 2000. Source: Office of the Deputy Prime Minister.
[3] Excluding London boroughs.

3.8   This enterprise gap in deprived areas is further compounded by a lower survival rate of businesses compared with more affluent areas. There is also a correlation between levels of entrepreneurial activity and income, with those on a low income almost half as likely to be involved in entrepreneurial activity compared with those in a higher income group.

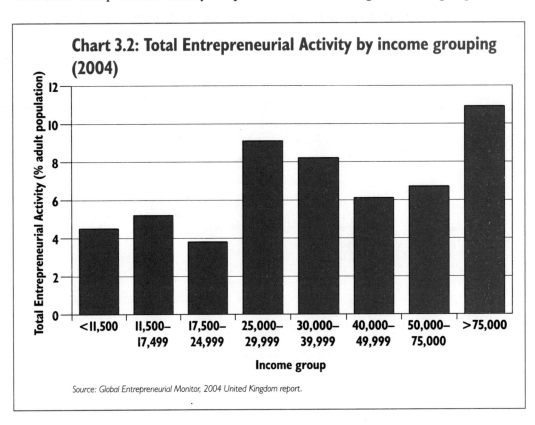

Chart 3.2: Total Entrepreneurial Activity by income grouping (2004)

Source: Global Entrepreneurial Monitor, 2004 United Kingdom report.

Enterprise and under-represented communities

Ethnic minorities **3.9** A high correlation also exists between deprived areas and geographical concentrations of ethnic minority groups. However, entrepreneurial activity differs markedly by ethnic group, with some minority groups having a far higher rate of entrepreneurial activity than others.

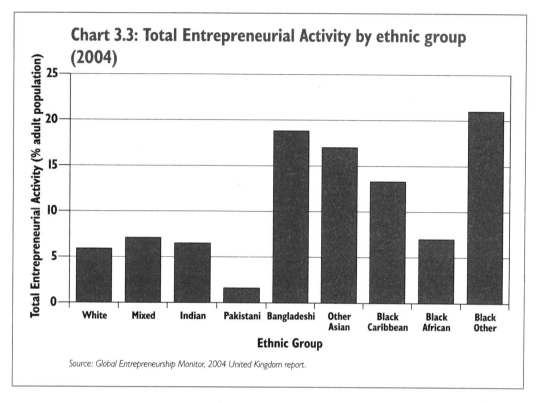

Chart 3.3: Total Entrepreneurial Activity by ethnic group (2004)

Source: Global Entrepreneurship Monitor, 2004 United Kingdom report.

3.10 This information shows that enterprise development efforts in deprived areas need to be well targeted at the most vulnerable or hard to reach groups in a deprived area. At the national level, the Government is committed to doing more to promote and support ethnic minority enterprise.

Box 3.2: Ethnic minority enterprise – National Employment Panel

In the 2004 Pre-Budget Report, the National Employment Panel (NEP), working with the Ethnic Minority Business Forum, were asked to report by Budget 2005 on measures to encourage employment, self-employment, and the growth of small business for ethnic and faith minority groups.

Several themes are brought-out strongly in NEP's work:

- **ethnic minority participation in the labour market is an economic issue:** in the next decade, 50 per cent of the growth in the workforce will come from ethnic minority communities;

- **it is unhelpful to generalise about ethnic minority employees or businesses:** there is considerable diversity within and between ethnic minority communities; and

- **serious and sustained political and business leadership is crucial:** this is important both to address the employment gap and to further encourage enterprise in ethnic minority communities.

More information on the work of NEP in this area can be found in Chapter 4 of the Budget 2005 document.

Female enterprise gap **3.11**   There is also a marked difference in the rate of entrepreneurial activity between the male and female population. This phenomenon is obviously not restricted to deprived areas, and indeed exists across all of the UK regions and nations.

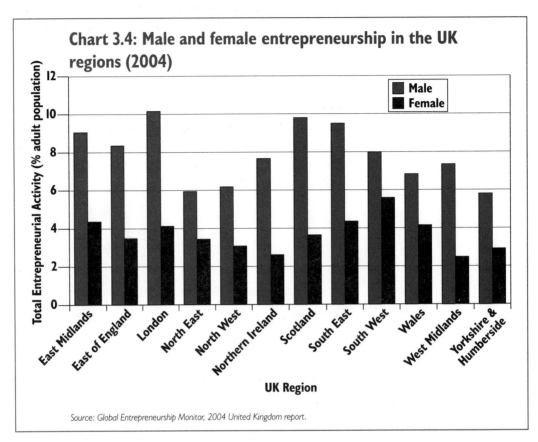

Chart 3.4: Male and female entrepreneurship in the UK regions (2004)

Source: Global Entrepreneurship Monitor, 2004 United Kingdom report.

3.12   Local enterprise development efforts – both in deprived and less deprived areas – should consider the scope for ensuring that entrepreneurial activity in the female population is catered for, to help address the significant under-utilisation of economic and social potential that this gender gap represents. This will require local strategies to be properly integrated with other relevant measures – such as appropriate provision of childcare – to ensure that this can become a reality.

3.13   Recognising these differences, the Government published a **Strategic Framework for Women's Enterprise** in 2003, which set out a long-term vision to create an environment and culture that encourages more women to start and grow businesses. Building on this, the Government welcomes the action plan recommended by the national **Women's Enterprise Panel** to significantly increase the proportion of UK businesses owned and run by women. The Government will work with RDAs and other stakeholders to take these recommendations forward.

Rationale for government intervention

3.14   A key element of the Government's enterprise policy is therefore the recognition that social attitudes, the business environment and specific market failures can present significantly higher barriers to enterprise within England's most deprived areas. Yet it is often the case that it is in these areas that the benefits of enterprise may have the greatest social impact and where there is economic potential lying unrealised. There are therefore two core reasons why the Government is committed to the aim of increasing the level of enterprise in England's most deprived areas:

1. **Efficiency**: deprived areas often face multiple market failures that discourage or inhibit both inward investment and enterprise, leading to the under-utilisation of factors of production. For example, if the highest rates of business activity in the UK were matched in deprived areas, there would be an extra 154,694 businesses in the UK – and if the UK matched US enterprise rates there would be an extra 1.9 million businesses. Correcting market failures in deprived areas can help develop the local economy and contribute to closing the enterprise gap.

2. **Equity**: concentrations of deprivation raise deep equity concerns in terms of access to jobs, opportunities for enterprise, and wealth creation. As well as being a key driver of productivity growth, successful enterprise and business growth form part of the bedrock of local communities, contributing to economic prosperity, higher living standards, and social cohesion.

BARRIERS IN DEPRIVED AREAS

3.15   Why are levels of enterprise lower in deprived areas? All areas encounter barriers to enterprise, but deprived areas can face barriers that are more acute, pervasive and persistent in nature. These barriers include issues related to:

*   access to finance;

*   business support and advice;

*   experience, skills and training;

*   enterprise culture;

*   institutional and administrative barriers; and

*   the business environment.

3.16   This section briefly considers each of these sets of barriers.

Access to finance

Start-up finance   **3.17**   Individuals in deprived areas can face difficulties in securing the initial investment in their business. This can be for many reasons, including having access to limited cash reserves and lack of collateral to act as security on a bank loan (often exacerbated by low house prices, lack of other financial assets, or prevalence of social-rented housing).

3.18   In addition, much initial investment in small business start-ups is often provided on an informal basis by friends and family of the aspiring entrepreneur. Again, in deprived areas these groups are also likely to have low incomes and savings and, while they may be willing, they may be unable to offer financial support. As a result, entrepreneurs in deprived areas may establish firms in sectors with low up-front capital requirements and minimal barriers to entry – often replicating existing businesses in the area, leading to severe competition and low rates of survival.

3.19   To boost the ability of potential entrepreneurs to access finance, the Government established a Community Investment Tax Relief (CITR) and the Phoenix Fund.

Box 3.3: Community Investment Tax Relief

The CITR, one of the five recommendations of the Social Investment Task Force, is available to individuals and corporate bodies investing in accredited Community Development Finance Institutions (CDFIs), which then in turn provide finance to qualifying enterprises, community projects or social enterprises.

The tax relief available to a prospective investor is 5 per cent per annum of the amount invested in the CDFI and may be claimed in the tax year in which the investment is made and in each of the four subsequent years.

Relationships with financial institutions

3.20   The relationships between banking and financial institutions and individuals in deprived areas can often be limited. Lack of an existing relationship and a limited history of banking can adversely affect the credit scoring of potential entrepreneurs. Individuals in deprived areas are twice as likely not to have a bank account, and the most recent Family Resources Survey in 2002-2003 showed that there were around 8 per cent or 1.9 million households in Great Britain without access to any kind of bank account, equating to one in twelve households or around 2.8 million adults.[5]

3.21   Geographical mapping of this group of 'unbanked' individuals shows a high correlation between areas of high financial exclusion and areas of deprivation. The Government has recently established a Financial Inclusion Fund worth £120 million over three years, supported by a Financial Inclusion Taskforce to tackle this issue.[6]

Box 3.4: Promoting financial inclusion

Following the HM Treasury publication *Promoting Financial Inclusion*, published alongside the 2004 Pre-Budget Report, the Government is establishing a Financial Inclusion Fund worth £120 million over three years to support initiatives to tackle financial exclusion. In particular, the Fund will support the Government's aims to increase access to forms of affordable credit and to see a significant increase in the capacity of free face-to-face money advice.

In addition, the Government has established a Financial Inclusion Taskforce to monitor progress against the objectives the Government has set, and to report to the Government on what more can be done to tackle financial exclusion.

Credit risk and information

3.22   Small and medium sized enterprises (SMEs) in deprived areas are often perceived by banks and financial institutions to have a higher credit risk due to fragile market demand, lack of capitalisation, and lack of access to collateral. In addition, there can be disproportionately high transaction costs for the lender in the cost of monitoring small loans to small or micro-businesses in what are perceived to be 'risky' markets.

3.23   This can be compounded by information asymmetries, as the potential entrepreneur possesses more information about the prospects of the new business than the lending institution. In deprived areas this may be exacerbated by a lack of experience among some lenders in lending to small businesses in deprived areas, with less understanding of their borrowing needs and performance.

---

[5] HM Treasury (2004a).

[6] *Ibid.*

3.24   The normal response of lending institutions to the extra cost of lending to SMEs would be to raise interest rates on loans. However, this would have the effect of pricing-out lower-risk borrowers and leaving an unprofitable subset of higher risk borrowers. To avoid this and to minimise exposure to what is perceived as unacceptable risk, lending institutions can sometimes set an upper limit on the amount available to borrow – thereby rationing credit to SMEs perceived as high risk. Credit rationing can be said to occur where a project which would yield positive private financial returns, after paying the costs of funding, fails to attract sufficient external finance.[7]

Social and financial returns   **3.25**   One further barrier to the financing of enterprise in deprived areas is the lack of attention paid to the social return on investment as well as the financial returns on investment. Enterprise – and social enterprise in particular – can generate many positive externalities to the wider community (such as wealth creation and multiplier effects), but these are not taken into account in decisions by lenders.

3.26   Social enterprises can also be misunderstood by lenders because of their perceived 'non-profit' status. However, social enterprises can be viable and sustainable businesses as they generate profit, but choose to reinvest these profits for the benefit of the wider community. The Government published Social Enterprise: a strategy for success in 2002 to raise the profile and understanding of social enterprises in the wider economy.

Box 3.5: Understanding social enterprise

A social enterprise can be defined as *"a business with primarily social objectives whose surpluses are principally reinvested for that purpose in the business of in the community, rather than being driven by the need to maximise profit for shareholders and owners."*[1]

Social Enterprise: a strategy for success – was published by the Department of Trade and Industry (DTI) in 2002, setting-out the vision for dynamic and sustainable social enterprise. The social enterprise strategy outlines the three key components in achieving this vision: creating an enabling environment; making social enterprises better businesses; and establishing the value of social enterprise.

To this end, DTI has published a short, good practice guide to help regional and local bodies collect comparable data on social enterprise, whether as part of a focussed study on social enterprise, or wider research into the social economy or business community. **Collecting Data on Social Enterprise: a guide to good practice** draws out the recommendations contained in the detailed research report, **Guidance on Mapping Social Enterprise**, commissioned by DTI in 2003. Based on the experience of 33 studies and extensive consultation with the social enterprise sector, the report and short guide are designed to be of practical use, encouraging the creation of a common core of knowledge that can be added to by innovative investigation of different aspects of the social enterprise sector.

[1] Department of Trade and Industry (2002b).

---

[7] HM Treasury (1999).

Business support and advice

Information and institutional gaps

3.27   While business support services are available in many deprived areas, their effectiveness can be limited by misconceptions – about who it is for, what is available, and how much it costs. These misconceptions can be caused by a lack of information available to potential entrepreneurs, a general lack of signposting, marketing and communication of support services, and no clear and understandable 'offer' of support that is guaranteed in every area.

3.28   In addition, there can be confusion over which organisation to approach to access business support – from Business Link, the Prince's Trust, Enterprise Agencies, to the local authority – each of which may or may not have the expertise or skills to meet the particular needs of the entrepreneur.

3.29   Related to this, there can also be a risk that potential entrepreneurs 'fall between the gaps' in the support services available. This can sometimes happen during the 'handover' of the entrepreneur between agencies with aligning remits. The Government has therefore committed to ensuring high quality support services, comprising business to business networks, brokerage and specialist services in every area.

Approachability and appropriateness

3.30   Some also hold the view that some support services are not as approachable as they might be for some individuals in deprived communities. In particular, ethnic minorities may not be catered for by business support services in a manner that is culturally sensitive. Irrespective of the evidence, if the *perception* exists that business support services are not as approachable as they should be, it has a significant negative effect on the ability of business support agencies to operate and meet their targets effectively.

3.31   Similarly, some business support services are seen as inappropriate for certain types of enterprise, with little institutional experience or understanding relevant to the differing experiences of these organisations – particularly with regard to social enterprise.

Box 3.6: Meeting the needs of local businesses in Birmingham

Business Link Birmingham and Solihull recognise the importance of meeting the specific needs of businesses in their community. They realised that conventional advertising of their services, like emails and newsletters, were not reaching all businesses, particularly ethnic minority businesses or those in deprived areas. When they asked traders about the help they needed, development officers for their areas was always top of the list.

In response to the needs of local businesses, Business Link Birmingham have recruited three front-line development offices who provide a human element to contact by getting out and about, and talking with businessmen and traders about their concerns. The officer will then go and find the people who can help in the council, the police, Business Link, or wherever assistance is available. This helps to highlight the needs and concerns of the traders and businesses and bring them to the attention of the service providers. The service providers can be told what sort of help is needed and can develop the appropriate services.

Geographical coverage **3.32** It is also true that while the coverage of business support providers is generally good, there remain geographical gaps that can have an effect on the levels of entrepreneurship – particularly in the cases when there is no business support provision within a deprived area. However, even when a business support provider does exist to serve the deprived area it may not actually be located within the area, and lack of suitable transport links can mean that the business support coverage is not as effective as it could be.

Experience, skills and training

Prior skills and work experience **3.33** Entrepreneurs tend to gather business ideas from previous work history (80 per cent of entrepreneurs create businesses based on previous work experience).[8] In particular, previous experience in the sector of the economy in which the entrepreneur is starting a business is crucial to the probability of survival of that business.

3.34 In deprived areas, the pool of potential entrepreneurs is more likely to contain individuals with a limited work history, and a greater likelihood of experience in low-technology sectors. This means that business proposals are less likely to be viable, or are likely to be for businesses which would operate in similar local markets and come under intense competition – with the consequent impact on likely survival rates.

'Mix' of skills **3.35** In addition, the ability of a prospective entrepreneur to start and run a business successfully depends in large part on the skills they have – and their ability to draw-up a suitable and effective business plan. Starting and running a business requires a broad set or 'mix' of skills, ranging from basic skills to managerial, financial and accounting, marketing skills, and often technical skills (especially in new, or high-technology industries).

3.36 It is quite rare for an aspiring entrepreneur to have the correct mix of skills – irrespective of whether or not they are from a deprived area – and there needs to be a certain degree of training, both formal and informal, to build the entrepreneur's skills over time. However, in deprived areas educational attainment is generally lower, meaning that there can be an even greater need to build the correct mix of skills to better enable enterprise development. At the same time, there may be a lack of formal training opportunities within the deprived area, holding back the development of skills of potential entrepreneurs.

Box 3.7: Continuing Education and Training Service in Croydon

The Croydon Council Continuing Education and Training Service (CETS) Business Start-up Programme provides highly practical "hands-on" courses designed to help aspiring entrepreneurs from deprived areas in the north of Croydon to write a business plan that will pass muster with commercial recipients. The nine-day courses spread over nine weeks include market research, marketing, legalities, raising finance, taxation, cashflow planning, book-keeping/accounts, networking, and mentoring. CETS also offer an after-care service for those who have started their businesses.

In nine years, over 900 students (80 per cent black and ethnic minority (BME) and 55 per cent women) have completed the course, which also helps participants to consider other career options with their new set of skills. Over 320 business started through CETS are known to be still trading.

---

[8] Fielden *et al* (2000) in OECD (2003).

Enterprise culture

Cultural barriers   **3.37**   Individuals in deprived areas may have particular cultural needs that, if not appreciated and catered for, can become a barrier to entrepreneurship. For example, linguistic barriers can create a significant barrier to the interaction with business support agencies and the ability to deal effectively with other public institutions.

Box 3.8: BME business outreach support

Croydon Council was instrumental in supporting the formation of SLEMBA (South London Ethnic Minority Business Association) over seven years ago to extend business support to reach people in deprived areas, and primarily BME entrepreneurs. They operate through localised workshops and training sessions, business briefings etc., and through advice, mentoring and signposting. The aim is to encourage hard to reach groups to use existing support services.

With cultural credibility to operate as an intermediary with marginalised communities, SLEMBA has been pivotal in facilitating access to business information and support, with emphasis on capacity building through skills development. This is achieved in association with partner organisations and programmes promoted through government funding streams (e.g. Learning and Skills Council and Single Regeneration Budget).

They target an average of about 200 business reviews per annum, recording perceived needs and making referrals to appropriate business support partners. This work also involves the building of an electronic database (over 500 records) as a means of sustaining contact, and for marketing opportunities and information of practical value to 'remote' businesses.

Role models   **3.38**   Effective role models are crucial to the development of a strong enterprise culture. Existing successful local entrepreneurs in deprived areas can become key role models for others to try and emulate or imitate. People who know an entrepreneur are more than twice as likely to enter business as those who do not.[9] Therefore, an absence of successful role models in deprived areas could have a knock-on effect on the overall levels of enterprise within that area.

3.39   Role models are very important in tackling issues of motivation and confidence, especially for those who have suffered from a protracted period of unemployment and are unlikely to enter business without being inspired to do so by someone else. The confidence and motivational effect of successful entrepreneurial role models should therefore not be underestimated.

---

[9] Reynolds et al (2001) in OECD (2003).

> **Box 3.9: Enterprising Britain Awards**
>
> On 28th June 2004 the Chancellor of the Exchequer launched the *Enterprising Britain Awards* – a competition to find the 'British city of Enterprise'. This competition celebrates and recognises enterprise achievement throughout the regions – creating 'geographical role models'.
>
> This competition, which operates on an annual basis, has two distinct stages: a regional nomination stage, with one candidate chosen from each region and devolved administration; and a nationwide competition between the regional nominations, where a panel of entrepreneurs and business-women choose the overall national winner.
>
> Sherwood Energy Village in Ollerton, Nottinghamshire won the inaugural Enterprising Britain competition – out of 11 other regional finalists. Ollerton, a former coalfield area, was announced as the national winner by the Chancellor of the Exchequer at the 'Advancing Enterprise' conference in London in February 2005.

Social capital 3.40   As discussed in Chapter 2, social capital – both social networks and trust between and within communities – can have a real impact on levels of entrepreneurial activity. In deprived areas, individuals are likely to be constrained by low levels of social capital, either through community breakdown, lack of community institutions or assets, poor access to suitable transport, or access to new information and communications technology. Building role models and increasing community cohesion can therefore raise social capital and impact upon levels of entrepreneurial activity.

Institutional and administrative barriers

Transition from benefits 3.41   Individuals in deprived areas may be more likely to experience a transition from benefits when starting or taking a job in a new business. This transition can be a daunting prospect for a number of reasons:

- the perception of a 'loss' of benefits (council tax benefit, housing benefit, job seekers allowance etc);

- the concern of possible delays or gaps in income;

- the administrative task involved ('form filling'); and

- misunderstanding or confusion over eligibility for in-work benefits.

3.42   As part of wider moves to continuously improve the benefits system, the Government has worked to promote and extend the Test Trading Allowance – an option to encourage and support recipients of Job Seekers Allowance, Income Support of Incapacity Benefit wishing to move into self-employment.

Government regulations 3.43   The costs of registering a new business are negatively related to enterprise creation.[10] Small businesses feel the impact of government regulations more acutely than larger businesses – new businesses often have only one or two members of staff, and dealing with the administrative burden of a diverse set of regulations can divert valuable time and effort from issues of management and financial security. The Government has done much since 1997 to reduce the administrative and regulatory burden on business, but is clear that more can be done.

---

[10] Djankov *et al* (2000) in OECD (2003).

Institutions **3.44** The Social Exclusion Unit Report *Jobs and Enterprise in Deprived Areas* recognised that businesses and entrepreneurs have to deal with a wide array of public and non-public institutions and can often suffer if the efforts, contracts and responsibilities of these institutions are not effectively joined-up at the local level.[11] The need to ensure local efforts are joined-up is even more important in deprived areas, where there are other barriers that the aspiring entrepreneur has to deal with.

3.45 Efforts to promote and develop enterprise in deprived areas therefore need to be coherent and comprehensive, joining-up efforts, funds, and strategies. Key to this is enhancing the role of local authorities in pursuing and co-ordinating enterprise development activities.

The business environment

3.46 A final barrier to enterprise is the quality of the physical and social business environment in which new, or inward-investing businesses have to operate.

Crime **3.47** Residents of deprived areas are more likely to be the victims of crime than people who live in other areas of the UK. Small businesses located in deprived areas are also vulnerable to crime – the *Annual Small Business Survey 2003* showed that about a third of small employers had been the victim of at least one crime in the previous 12 months. Crime and the fear of crime are therefore regularly cited as key reasons for companies deciding not to invest in deprived areas. Apart from deterring businesses, crime also forces firms to divert valuable resources from growing the business into 'unproductive' assets such as expensive security systems.

Business **3.48** Finding suitable and available premises for new business start-ups can be a particular
premises problem for entrepreneurs in deprived areas. Premises in deprived areas can often be the wrong size, in the wrong location, or unsuitable for the business concerned (for example, a business services firm will need a very different type of premises from a small, manufacturing-oriented firm, or from a firm in the retail sector). The Government has funded feasibility studies for business incubators in the 88 Neighbourhood Renewal areas that are also Enterprise Areas, and is introducing a Business Premises Renovation Allowance in Enterprise Areas to provide support to bring under-utilised business premises back into use.

Taking a local approach

3.49 However, just as there are geographical variations across England's regions and sub-regions with regard to enterprise activity, barriers to enterprise in deprived areas vary from one local community to another (from ex-coalfield areas, inner-city areas, coastal resorts, to peripheral estates, or rural areas). Therefore, solutions will need to be tailored to specific local priorities and needs. Local authorities – with the support of regional institutions – are well placed to pursue local enterprise development strategies that can better target specific needs with locally-developed and locally-appropriate measures.

3.50 Efforts to remove barriers to, and promote enterprise will, therefore, require both a general and a specific approach. The remainder of this chapter therefore focuses on the efforts made at the central government level to promote enterprise in deprived areas – through the Phoenix Fund and the Enterprise Areas package. Chapter 5 then introduces a new proposal to support and resource complementary local efforts to develop enterprise and economic activity in deprived areas.

---

[11] ODPM (2004).

THE GOVERNMENT'S APPROACH

3.51   Government policy on enterprise in deprived areas has been driven by the original Policy Action Team 3 1999 report *Enterprise and Social Exclusion*.

Box 3.10: Policy Action Team 3: Enterprise and Social Exclusion

The Government's interest and policy on enterprise in deprived areas has been driven by the original work of the Policy Action Team (PAT) 3 – part of the wider development of the National Strategy for Neighbourhood Renewal. The main finding of the report was summarised as follows:

"Our single most important finding is simply that promoting enterprise in deprived communities does not get the attention it deserves – whether from the different parts of central government, or from the diversity of local and regional institutions, or from private sector banks and other firms. There is more that can be done by all these parties towards goals that should be common – building communities with stronger local markets, and giving everyone with the potential to succeed in business the opportunity to do so."

3.52   The Government recognises that no deprived area will ever be turned-around if shortages of jobs, local services, and enterprise are not addressed, and it is in these communities that the benefits of enterprise will have the greatest social impact. The economic challenge is therefore to rebuild livelihoods and restore robust local markets. Sustainable neighbourhood renewal will not happen without enterprise development, but on the other hand, enterprise development will be of only marginal relevance unless it is part of a wider neighbourhood renewal strategy designed to tackle the range of problems that deprived areas face.

3.53   In response to the PAT 3 report, the Government established the Phoenix Fund to support enterprise in deprived areas through improving access to finance and levels and quality of business support services.

Box 3.11: Phoenix Fund

The Phoenix Fund was launched in November 1999 in response to the PAT 3 report *Enterprise and Social Exclusion*. It tackles issues of access to business support and finance which often represent particular difficulties for people in disadvantaged communities. The fund also promotes the creation of social enterprises. In particular, the fund has provided around £20 million worth of support to Community Development Finance Institutions (CDFIs) to enable them to further develop their core activities of providing finance and associated support to enterprises that would have a positive impact on disadvantaged communities but are unable to access the finance they require from conventional sources. A wide range of innovative projects are also supported through the Phoenix Development Fund, developing new approaches to providing business support, especially for under-presented groups.

More information on the Phoenix Fund can be found at: www.sbs.gov.uk/phoenix

---

3.54   In addition, the Enterprise Areas package announced in the 2002 Pre-Budget Report, aims to help address the range of barriers to enterprise, economic activity, and opportunity for all, and draw-together the range of policy tools available to local and regional organisations to tackle the problems their communities face.

Box 3.12: Enterprise Areas

Enterprise Areas are the 1,997 most deprived areas of the UK. Currently there are a range of measures to tackle the market failures and barriers to enterprise that can be most severe in Enterprise Areas. This 'toolkit' includes:

- **Community Investment Tax Relief to improve access to finance for small business through CDFI;**

- **Bridges Community Development Venture Fund, a £40 million fund from Government and the private sector to provide venture capital funding;**

- **enhanced and targeted advice and support from HM Revenue and Customs;**

- **a wide range of innovative projects, through the Phoenix Development Fund, developing new approaches to providing business support, especially for under-presented groups; and**

- **Business Premises Renovation Allowance (following State Aid clearance).**

More information on Enterprise Areas is set out in Annex A.

3.55   The Government believes there is more that can be done to tackle the enterprise gap in deprived areas, and build a new approach to enterprise development as an economic development strategy – supported by a step-change in commitment of public resources over the long-term. In particular, the Government believes that:

- local areas need **local solutions** to enterprise development;

- **targeting** the areas with both a real identifiable need and opportunity at the national level is fraught with difficulty;

- efforts on enterprise development need to be **integrated** with other local efforts – on public services and neighbourhood renewal – and other local institutions;

- enterprise development should be an aim shared by a **strong partnership** of both public sector agencies, businesses and the third sector at the local level; and

- the **provision of resources** to support such an approach needs to recognise the **long-term** nature of enterprise development.

3.56 The Government will therefore pursue 'three pillars' of support for enterprise development:

1. **National:** tackling certain key enterprise development issues at the national level through an ongoing commitment to building on the Enterprise Areas package where either economies of scale are required, or where issues are common across many areas.

2. **Regional:** devolving to the regional level new responsibilities for the delivery of Business Link and the Phoenix Fund, to enable an integrated approach to business support.

3. **Local:** building-on support through the Neighbourhood Renewal Strategy, providing significant commitment to support locally-appropriate plans for enterprise development through a Local Enterprise Growth Initiative (LEGI) worth £50 million in 2006-2007, rising to £150 million per year by 2008-2009, subject to the 2006 Spending Review.

3.57 Details of the proposed LEGI are outlined in Chapter 5, along with the key questions for consultation. The development of the LEGI proposal was informed by a set of key, high-level principles, briefly set-out in Chapter 4, that have been developed following extensive research, evaluation of international policies, and discussions with many key stakeholders in local government, the regional development agencies, and business.

4

DEVELOPING A PRINCIPLED APPROACH

SUMMARY

4.1   In developing the new proposal for a Local Enterprise Growth Initiative (LEGI), the Government is committed to following a principled approach on the basis of past experience, research and an ongoing dialogue with key stakeholders in local government, regional institutions, and the business community.

4.2   The proposal for the LEGI is therefore based on a set of six key principles: effective targeting (to ensure people living in deprived areas benefit); effective solutions (to address the fundamental barriers to growth); significant commitment (of resources over the long-term); strong local partnerships (with business and the wider community); integration (with broader regeneration efforts); and evaluation and evidence building (to inform continuous improvement and the development of future policy).

PRINCIPLE 1 – EFFECTIVE TARGETING

Most deprived areas   **4.3**   The 2004 Social Exclusion Report *Jobs and Enterprise in Deprived Areas* highlights the significant additional disadvantage faced by people living in the most deprived areas and the extent of spatial inequalities across a range of social and economic outcomes. The extent of floor targets and willingness to focus extra resource on the most deprived areas demonstrates the Government's commitment to improving the outcomes for individuals living in areas of greatest deprivation and narrowing the gap between the richest and poorest areas.

Benefit local people   **4.4**   However, policies that target the most deprived areas don't always benefit the people living in those areas, for example, if a large inward investor locates in a deprived area but recruits a large majority of employees from outside that area. There are methods to ensure the benefits of enterprise development strategies in deprived areas are 'internalised' to benefit local people.

> **Box 4.1: French Urban Free Zones – targeting local people**
>
> The French Urban Free Zones (ZFUs) give small and medium-sized companies tax and social security relief, but restrict that relief to companies who reserve one third of their jobs for local inhabitants. This requirement does not seem to have been overly restrictive as the minimum local recruitment level was exceeded, the rate of new company formation was seven times higher in the ZFUs than in the surrounding areas, and the number of wage earning employees in the area quadrupled.

4.5   This evidence highlights the importance of ensuring that local inhabitants benefit from local enterprise development activities. Therefore, it is crucial to partner place-based enterprise measures with place-based people strategies at the local level, linking people in need to the opportunities being created.

Areas with **4.6**   The second component of targeting efforts is selecting the most deprived areas that
opportunity also have potential to benefit from enterprise development. Note that this does not mean
selecting areas that will improve without the measure. Indices based purely on residential
measures of deprivation can present certain limitations in this context as residential
deprivation says little about the lack or otherwise of local business activity. For example, the
Office of the Deputy Prime Minister (ODPM) *Underserved Markets* project (Chapter 2) was
able to show investors that deprived areas can present significant untapped business
opportunities and underserved markets.

4.7   Local authorities therefore need to be empowered to use local knowledge to select the
deprived areas that would benefit most from enterprise development activities. These areas
may well be those that present the competitive advantages or opportunities outlined in
Chapter 2.

PRINCIPLE 2 – EFFECTIVE SOLUTIONS

4.8   Deprived areas face significant and entrenched difficulties that cannot be changed
overnight. However, effective and well implemented solutions can address local barriers and
achieve real change over the long-term. To effectively achieve long-term economic
development of the most deprived areas, policy solutions must be:

- **locally effective** – policy solutions must address the underlying barriers or
  market failures that are inhibiting the area and its people;

- **effectively implemented** – utilising local knowledge of the area to ensure that
  the policy solution is locally appropriate; and

- **high awareness and marketing** – businesses must either be aware of the
  programme, or of the impact it is having, for it to have an impact on their
  location, growth, and start-up decisions

Effective **4.9**   A long-term solution must address the underlying disadvantage of an area to enable
a positive cycle of improvement. Measures that address market failures that are discouraging
businesses from locating, growing, or starting-up in an area are likely to be the most cost-
effective and are least likely to introduce distortions with wider economic costs. Examples of
areas where there are likely to be clear market failure rationale include: provision of business
advice; training; access to finance; provision of flexible business premises; addressing
inaccurate and negative perceptions of the area; and helping with crime prevention and
security costs.

Locally **4.10**   Locally flexible solutions are necessary because deprived areas are not uniform and,
appropriate therefore, a 'one size fits all' policy solution will not meet the needs of all areas. Local areas,
and their strengths and weaknesses, are only fully understood at the local level – by the
community, businesses, and local government – so effective solutions need to be guided by
local knowledge wherever possible.

Effectively implemented   **4.11**   Effective and long-term enterprise development solutions require effective implementation, providing the right incentives, and minimising adverse side effects.

4.12   One aspect of this is utilising local knowledge to ensure that measures build on and are integrated with broader regeneration efforts. The French ZFUs and the evaluations of the UK City Challenge suggest that an allocation process can be used to ensure that funding is provided to those who will make best use of it, and to ensure that they have a well thought-through implementation strategy.

4.13   Effective implementation is more likely if new incentives complement, rather than conflict with, existing incentives. As an example, in the US extra revenue from business rates derived from a regenerated area is retained by the city government, incentivising the local authorities to facilitate the objectives of Empowerment Zones. This incentive on local authorities to focus on business growth is also being introduced in the UK through the Business Growth Incentive.

4.14   In addition, the implementation of policies should not add to the burden of red-tape on local businesses. Red-tape costs discourage businesses from seeking support and reduce the impact of any policies put in place.

Marketing and awareness   **4.15**   A successful business focused regeneration policy must be known about and understood by businesses, and the cost to the business of using the policy must not outweigh its benefit. For example, the French ZFUs are well known and understood, and carry prestige – due to the size of the relief and community buy-in to the bidding process.

PRINCIPLE 3 – SIGNIFICANT COMMITMENT

4.16   As noted in Principle 2, the most deprived areas face significant and multiple difficulties that are not easily tackled. Therefore, effective and long-term solutions may require interventions that are intense and may have to be relatively long-term. The evaluation of the UK City Challenge programme indicated that the five years of funding provided was not always long enough to tackle the areas of most significant disadvantage.

4.17   Evidence suggests that more intensive efforts can have an extra impact through creating a critical-mass or dynamic and raising policy awareness among businesses. To effect significant behavioural change among businesses, the perceived benefit of the measure must outweigh the perceived cost to the business to change behaviour (for example, relocating to a deprived area).

4.18   Certainty is a further element that is important to business decisions, as businesses are less likely to commit heavily in an area if future benefits are uncertain. Businesses should therefore have certainty over clearly specified time horizons.

PRINCIPLE 4 – STRONG LOCAL PARTNERSHIPS

4.19   Policies must be designed to ensure partnership between local and regional agencies, central government organisations, and crucially with a strong lead from local authorities, business and the community. The critical partners in a local area regeneration strategy are:

- local authorities;

- local businesses and the local community, for whom the intervention is intended to benefit; and

- agencies that have cross-cutting economic development or regeneration initiatives that impact on the area or its inhabitants, such as the Learning and Skills Council, regional development agencies (RDAs) central government as well as social enterprises and the third sector.

Local community **4.20**   One of the problems many deprived areas face is that they can be transit areas that people leave as soon as they have the means to do so.[1] To transform an area requires building a community that residents and businesses feel part of and want to stay in, by changing the aspects of the area that matter to that community. Local involvement can help to form a sense of community and to ensure that the policy benefits individuals living in the area.

Business **4.21**   An enterprise development policy must be attractive to the kinds of businesses that **partnerships** might locate or start-up in that area. To ensure barriers faced by local businesses are addressed effectively the views of these businesses must be sought and fed into the local policy-making process, often with businesses taking a central role in that process. In some cases the obstacles identified by businesses are as simple as having an ATM on the local high street or taking action against anti-social behaviour.

4.22   Sometimes, businesses can be better placed to implement certain policy solutions such as business mentoring, neighbourhood watch schemes, or local business networking activities.

Box 4.2: Involving businesses in regeneration - East London Business Alliance[1]

There is a history of business involvement in Newham, and the Business Broker project has acted as a platform to take this to a new level. Despite high levels of deprivation, huge strides are being made in the regeneration of the borough to capitalise on developments such as the redevelopment of Stratford City and Silvertown Quays, the expansion of transport links, the Thames Gateway bridge and the prospect of the 2012 Olympics.

The Business Broker project has involved a wide range of local, City of London and Canary Wharf companies, levering-in support for projects and initiatives, for example a Social Enterprise Support programme partnering senior business leaders with community entrepreneurs. Through the broker projects, EDF Energy has become involved in providing a range of support to the West Ham and Plaistow New Deal for Communities project from mentoring to IT skills. Other activities have included a programme of business mentoring with the Metropolitan Police, business support to general practitioners and the Health Service, and working in partnership with the Education Business Partnership.

[1] Educe ltd CEA (2005)

---

[1] North, Smallbone, Lyon, and Potts (2003) Office of the Deputy Prime Minister report.

Local government and regional institutions

4.23 The third set of critical partners in local enterprise development are the public institutions that are involved in broader regeneration policies, including RDAs, Government Offices, local authorities, Job Centre Plus, and Learning Skills Councils.

4.24 Strong commitment from all partners has been shown to be a critical factor in the success of similar programmes. For example, the 2000 Department of the Environment, Transport and the Regions report *Final Evaluation of City Challenge* found a significant component of programme success depended on each element of the partnership contributing strongly. In particular, effective performance of the partnership depended significantly on having strong community involvement; effective partnership working; integration with neighbouring initiatives; and effective delivery and forward planning.[2]

4.25 The challenge is how to ensure strong partnership involvement and commitment across such a wide range of organisations. Stakeholders have suggested a number of elements are important in achieving successful partnership performance:

- structures to ensure government works well together;
- increasing local flexibility to create common objectives;
- earning the trust and support of local businesses;
- improving information on which to base decisions; and
- a robust performance framework to assess progress against objectives.

Box 4.3: Working together locally - Hartlepool Borough Council, New Deal for Communities, Business Link, and local businesses

In 2003, Hartlepool Borough Council and New Deal for Communities commissioned a report into business incubation within Hartlepool. The main recommendation of the report was that there was the need to provide additional "physical" incubation as well as an "incubation system" to sit alongside it. This has initially resulted in UK Steel Enterprise agreeing to build a new Innovation Centre in the Town, with assistance of TV Partnership funding (Single Programme). In addition, the Council operated incubator, Brougham Enterprise Centre, is to be extended and updated to better serve the needs of the new business community. Hartlepool Borough Council has also begun to roll out the incubation system in partnership with the local Business Link, which includes:

- better networking between businesses both in terms of inter-trading and offering mutual support and informal mentoring – in conjunction with a group of entrepreneurs ("Enterprising Hartlepool") who are driving forward this aspect of the strategy. They have held events where businesses have round table opportunities to sell themselves (like 'speed-dating' for businesses) and have also spoken at events where potential new start businesses have been in attendance;

- a new project looking at "Access to Markets" which aims to encourage new businesses to look beyond the region for customers - this is a joint project with Business Link's International Trade Team and includes some financial assistance; and

- the Council are also looking to develop an "Access to Finance" project within this system, finance being another area where businesses struggle in the early days.

---

[2] *Final Evaluation of City Challenge*, Department of the Environment, Transport and the Regions (2000).

PRINCIPLE 5 – AN INTEGRATED APPROACH

4.26   The best prospects for economic development are often provided by policies that match interventions that target effective labour supply with effective labour demand. Many regeneration policies target labour supply capacity (such as skills or health policies), which business-focused economic development can make use of by stimulating labour demand. Therefore, enterprise development strategies are often most effective when:

- they are linked to policies that free up local labour supply and addresses other issues that are propagating disadvantage in the area such as crime, health, or housing; and

- they are combined with other regeneration strategies that combine to provide critical mass, as it takes significant interventions over long periods of time to regenerate the most deprived areas.

4.27   The advantages of integrating regeneration policies needs to set against the danger of losing focus and overloading those involved with bureaucracy. The US Empowerment Zone programme suggests programmes that attempt to cover diverse areas, ranging from housing and social services to business, dilutes the business focus of policies and reduces the impact on local economic activity.

PRINCIPLE 6 – EVALUATE AND BUILD EVIDENCE

4.28   One of the critical problems in developing policy in this area is the paucity of evidence on the effectiveness of various interventions. A number of programmes examined did not have evaluation and evidence gathering as a critical component. For example, because the US State Enterprise Zones were not set up to track the spending or the impact of the zones, the selection process in subsequent rounds was not informed by any better information than in the initial rounds.

4.29   Developing a policy with evaluation and evidence as a priority ensures that the policy can benefit from a continuous improvement process, and also helps in developing future policies.

5 LOCAL ENTERPRISE GROWTH INITIATIVE

SUMMARY

Aim 5.1   The Local Enterprise Growth Initiative will provide flexible, devolved investment in our most deprived areas – determined by the Neighbourhood Renewal Fund areas – to support locally-developed and owned proposals that pursue new or proven ways of stimulating economic activity and productivity through enterprise development. The LEGI will be worth £50 million in 2006-2007, rising to £150 million per year by 2008-2009, subject to confirmation in the 2006 Spending Review.

5.2   The national-level aim of the LEGI is:

"To release the productivity and economic potential of our most deprived local areas and their inhabitants through enterprise and investment – thereby boosting local incomes and employment opportunities."

Objectives 5.3   This high-level aim is supported by three outcomes:

1. To increase **total entrepreneurial activity** among the population in deprived local areas.

2. To support the **sustainable growth** – and reduce the failure rate – of locally-owned business in deprived local areas.

3. To attract appropriate **inward investment and franchising** into deprived areas, making use of local labour resources.

5.4   These three outcomes reflect the contribution that business start-ups, growth businesses, and inward investors make to both national-level productivity growth and local economic development in deprived areas – as set-out previously in Chapters 1 and 2. To ensure sustainability over the long-term, the LEGI will be focused on the fundamental issues and barriers that hold-back enterprise and growth.

Devolution 5.5   The LEGI will follow closely the principles of devolution, providing local institutions and communities with the authority and freedom to best determine the local needs, options and solutions for enterprise development in deprived areas. Within the three broad outcomes set-out above, there will be significant discretion to determine what the local priorities should be and how to tackle them – what indicators to aim for, what actions to pursue, and what local targets are needed.

5.6   Therefore, local authorities that are also Neighbourhood Renewal Fund areas will be free to develop their own locally-appropriate proposals for enterprise development, in partnership with business and the wider community, and apply to the Government Offices for LEGI support. Local authorities will be expected to consult their regional development agency (RDA) to ensure a proper fit of local proposals within the wider Regional Economic Strategy, which identifies long-term regional priorities for enterprise in deprived areas.

How will it work? 5.7   The resources provided by the LEGI will be targeted at in-depth interventions in local authority areas with both a need (measured by level of deprivation) and potential (business activity and opportunities). Therefore, local authorities that are designated as Neighbourhood Renewal Fund areas will be eligible for LEGI support. The aim of the LEGI is to make a long-term change, transforming local deprived areas by tackling the market failures that inhibit growth, making a change that is sustained beyond the life of the policy. The overall amount of resources will be divided between the English regions and held by the Government Offices.

5.8 Local authorities that are eligible for LEGI support will be able apply to their Government Office for resources to support their local enterprise development proposals. The Government Office will enter into a light-touch negotiation with the local authority – as part of the wider process associated with Local Area Agreements (LAAs) if one exists – to determine the relevant indicators and targets in return for the resources.

5.9 The LEGI resources will be channelled through a LAA (where one exists) in a dedicated fourth funding block, allowing local authorities to pool this and other economic development and enterprise funding streams in one place and use them in a flexible way to deliver the outcomes agreed. Where the LAA is a single pot, the LEGI will form part of that pot in the normal way. Where a Local Area Agreement does not exist, the process will happen in a similar way.

Resources **5.10** The Government is clear that the LEGI resources need to be targeted at a select number of deprived local areas in sufficient depth to make a long-term difference. Therefore, the Government expects to be able to support around 30 local authorities with Neighbourhood Renewal Fund areas with the current funding profile. Future rounds of the LEGI will be determined as part of future Spending Reviews.

5.11 Individual local authorities that are successful in applying for LEGI support should expect to receive a significant sum of money – anything between £2-10 million depending on the 'critical mass' of resources required in different areas. This level of funding will be available for these authorities for a significant period of time (anything from five to ten years) to support the local enterprise development proposals – illustrating the Government's significant commitment to reviving these local economies over the long-term.

Evidence **5.12** The local authority, as part of the wider LAA process (where relevant), will be responsible for performance monitoring and reporting to the Government Office, as necessary, against agreed indicators. Given the relative paucity of comparable evidence of what does and does not work in this area, one prime condition of LEGI support will be the development of and contribution to a better local and national evidence base to show the impact of enterprise development on deprived areas.

5.13 The remainder of this chapter discusses these points in more detail, and asks for views on key aspects of the proposal.

AIM AND OUTCOMES

5.14 The aim, outcomes and national-level indicators will be pre-defined to ensure the resources are used wisely and contribute to national goals expressed through the Public Service Agreement (PSA) framework, and also to reduce deadweight that might result from the fund displacing rather than complementing other existing funds. Within this broad framework, local areas will have significant discretion – as outlined in more detail later in this chapter.

Aim and outcomes

5.15   The LEGI contributes to a number of core government PSAs,[1] on:

- Neighbourhood Renewal (Office of the Deputy Prime Minister (ODPM) PSA 1)

- Enterprise (Department of Trade and Industry (DTI) PSA 6)

- Productivity (HM Treasury PSA 4)

- Employment (shared Department of Work and Pensions (DWP) and HM Treasury PSA)

- Regional growth (shared DWP, ODPM and HM Treasury PSA)

5.16   However, because of the obvious and important synergies between the LEGI and the development of sustainable communities, and also the practical day-to-day policy responsibility for local government and neighbourhood renewal, **the ODPM will be the lead department for the LEGI.**

Indicators

5.17   An important aspect of the LEGI will be the ability to track progress and also to develop the evidence base on enterprise development in deprived areas. As such, it is important to ensure indicators are in place to assess progress against the three core objectives of the LEGI. Local proposals should follow set milestones over time, tracking progress and ensuring efforts remain focussed on achieving results. **A core set of basic indicators, used in a consistent manner, will allow a national set of data to be developed to inform future policy development.** Table 5.1 suggests some indicators for each of the three outcomes.

> **Question 5.1:** Are the suggested indicators for the LEGI the right ones – are there others to consider? What can be, or is already, measured at the local level that can be used in this way?

5.18   Table 5.1 illustrates how the national aim of the LEGI cascades into outcomes, indicators and targets. The details in the top four rows of the table will be predetermined at the national level prior to the launch of the fund. The development of the detail set-out in the remaining rows of the table targets, evidence, local indicators and actions - would be subject to discretion of local authorities, working in close partnership with their RDA, local businesses and the wider community, before being negotiated and agreed with the Government Offices as part of the LAA process where one exists.

---

[1] Further detail on the Government's PSAs can be found in the PSA White Paper on the HM Treasury internet site.

Table 5.1: Detail of the Local Enterprise Growth Initiative

RELEVANT PSAs	Neighbourhood renewal – ODPM 1 Enterprise – DTI 6 Productivity – HMT 4 Employment – DWP 4 / HMT 5 Regions – HMT 6 / DTI 7 / ODPM 2		
AIM	*"To release the productivity and economic potential of our most deprived local areas through enterprise and investment – thereby boosting local incomes and employment opportunities"*		
OUTCOMES	1 To increase total entrepreneurial activity amongst the local population (START-UPS)	2 To support the sustainable growth, and reduce the failure, of locally-owned business (GROWTH)	3 To attract appropriate inward investors, making use of local labour resources (JOBS)
NATIONAL INDICATORS	• Total Entrepreneurial Activity rate (GEM) • VAT registrations	• Business failure rates • Insolvency levels • Labour productivity (output per worker)	• Employment rates • GDP per capita
TARGETS	Government Offices and LAs could negotiate and agree output measures for the headline objectives as part of the LAA process		
EVIDENCE	Development of a local evidence base to determine local needs, what mechanisms to pursue (see below) to meet the headline outcomes (see above) to learn lessons of what works and doesn't		
POSSIBLE LOCAL INDICATORS	• Increase female entrepreneurship • Increase ethnic minority entrepreneurship • Reduce fear of failure • Increase no. of people who see enterprise as a good career choice (esp. young people) • Shift business activity from informal to formal market • Increase access to informal and community investment	• Increase access to informal and community investment • Increase business skills e.g. management and financial skills • Increase coverage of effective business support and advice services	• Reduce negative perceptions of the local area among business community • Reduce unnecessary administrative and institutional barriers • Increase vocational skills and work experience of local labour • Increase franchised business activity and brand or 'anchor' institutions
EXAMPLE ACTIONS	• Business incubation units and centres • Establish local enterprise awards scheme • Enterprise events in schools • Support local community finance to provide microfinance to fledgling SMEs	• Increase no. of business mentors • Fund local enterprise agencies – 'a business support service on every high street' • Establish range of subsidised business management and finance courses / seminars	• Develop local 'business prospectus' • Survey local business on burdensome local regulations • Establish network of work experience placements in local businesses • Establish a Business Planning Zone

DEVOLUTION TO THE LOCAL LEVEL

5.19 As the table above illustrates, the local authority will have considerable freedom to choose the most appropriate manner of delivering these broad outcomes. This policy proposal has been guided by the principles of devolution set-out in previous Government publications.

Principles of devolution

5.20 The *Devolving Decision Making Review* explained that this Government's long-term objective has always been to match ambitious national standards with local autonomy and flexibility to maximise efficiency and equity.[2] This involves a significant and radical devolution of responsibilities from Whitehall to local institutions and communities and an evolution in the relationship between central government, local government, regional institutions and the front line.

5.21 Therefore, the LEGI proposal follows the principle that central government needs to maintain a strategic role, ensuring national standards are met and maintained, but allowing greater scope locally to determine other priorities and decide how best to deliver national outcomes.[3] **One of the key reforms introduced to allow greater devolution – and which will be utilised by this new proposal where possible – is the introduction of Local Area Agreements.**

Box 5.1: Local Area Agreements

LAAs simplify the number of additional funding streams from central government going into an area, help join up public services more effectively and allow greater flexibility for local solutions to local circumstances.

They will be agreements struck between Government, the local authority and its major delivery partners in an area (working through the Local Strategic Partnerships). The majority of 2005-2006 agreements are structured around three blocks: children and young people, safer and stronger communities, and healthier communities and older people. From 2006-2007, a fourth block will be added which will focus on economic development issues, except for those areas that have a single pot, where the LEGI will form an integral part of that pot.

LAAs will help devolve decision making, move away from a 'Whitehall knows best' philosophy and reduce bureaucracy. Also, they are one of the first products of the Government's Ten Year Vision strategy.

LAAs will be driven by the local authority with the local strategic partnership (to ensure engagement of local partners). Negotiations will be overseen by the respective Government Office and signed off by ministers.

Pilot LAAs are now underway in 21 areas. At the Sustainable Communities Summit 2005, the Deputy Prime Minister announced a further pilot phase of 40 agreements to be in place by April 2006.

Question 5.2: In areas without Local Area Agreements, what is the best way to ensure that the LEGI is integrated with and generates leverage from other related programmes?

---

[2] HM Treasury/Cabinet Office (2004).
[3] *Ibid.*

Developing local proposals

5.22   Making use of the flexibility provided locally, the local authorities designated as Neighbourhood Renewal Fund areas will be free to develop local proposals for enterprise development within a selected area within the local authority boundary (or jointly with another authority for a deprived area that crosses authority boundaries). **These proposals should ideally form part of the wider Community Strategy,** and should be used as the basis for application for LEGI support. Key to the development of such proposals is the need to:

- work closely with local partners and the RDAs;

- develop a local evidence base to inform decision-making;

- determine both the appropriate local indicators to pursue and the actions (or policies) required to meet them;

- integrate with wider efforts including neighbourhood renewal; and

- set challenging outcome focused targets to incentivise delivery and secure value for money.

5.23   These factors will be considered by Government Offices when assessing individual applications for LEGI support.

Work with partners   5.24   A key element of developing and delivering proposals for effective local enterprise development that are worthy of LEGI support will be **engaging with key local stakeholders, particularly the business community,** but also other local or sub-regional public institutions with related and complementary programmes. Government Offices will also expect to see some involvement of the local community where relevant.

5.25   Any local proposals in the field of economic development will need to fit with the broader Regional Economic Strategy (RES) developed by the RDA. **Local authorities should therefore work in partnership with the RDAs,** not only to ensure there is congruence with the RES, but that complementarities and synergies are taken advantage of, combining resources where possible and appropriate.

> **Question 5.3: How could the Local Strategic Partnerships ensure sufficient business involvement in the development of local proposals for enterprise development and growth?**

Develop local evidence base   5.26   Evidence on what types of enterprise development proposals work and what do not is vitally important to the development of local proposals that will make a real, long-term difference. Evidence can both help continuously improve existing policies and help develop better future policies. However, current evidence on the impact of enterprise in deprived areas is limited, and **local authorities should therefore explain in their applications for LEGI support how they will gather evidence** at the outset to inform local policies, and also how their work will help build and contribute to the development of a greater understanding and evidence base more broadly.

> **Question 5.4:** How can the LEGI best co-ordinate and consolidate evidence and lessons learnt from the resources used?

Determine appropriate indicators 5.27 Once the local authority has gathered sufficient evidence, it will need to determine what local indicators should be pursued that are most important locally, but also contribute to the three core national outcomes. For example, where one area may choose to target levels of entrepreneurship among particular ethnic minority groups, another area may choose to attempt to reduce the fear of debt and fear of failure – both context specific but equally important in increasing overall levels of entrepreneurial activity.

Consider appropriate actions 5.28 The actions – or policies – that the local area pursues will obviously be guided by the indicators it decides to pursue. The LEGI will provide great flexibility to local areas to pursue different policies by providing 100 per cent resource funding – allowing the local authority to borrow to invest, or fund short-term projects.

> **Box 5.2: Rural economic development in Cumbria – a context specific approach**
>
> Rural Regeneration Cumbria (RRC) is a joint initative of the North West RDA and Cumbria County Council established in 2003. RRC is designed to regenerate Cumbria's rural economy where Gross Value Added (GVA) is at 77 per cent of the EU average, the lowest of any area in England. RRC encompasses a wide range of programmes, two of which are outlined below.
>
> **Rural Womens Network (RWN)** - aims to help women in Cumbria maximise the contribution they make to the economy through enterprise support and the development of personal and workplace skills. The services provided by RWN include: disseminating information on opportunities for successes by women; creating networks within which women can share experience and learn from their peers; providing opportunities to enhance both personal and business skills with accredited courses; and providing support and advice in business planning and development.
>
> The initiative has proven to be highly effective and has delivered impressive results: with over 2,600 members receiving information; 798 women taking part in networking opportunities; 348 women taking part in training events (personal development and business skills); 400 women receiving training bursaries; 366 receiving one-to-one business advice; 65 business start ups; and 100 jobs created.
>
> **Farming Connect Cumbria (FCC)** - is a programme from 2004–2008 providing integrated business and environmental advice to over 1,500 Cumbrian farming businesses backed up by a series of core farm investment grants to improve farm technical efficiency, environmental outputs, and succession planning. Many of these farms are situated in rural disadvantaged areas. FCC provides free business and environmental advice across the farm income spectrum to assist farmers in striving towards true sustainability. Since its inception in July 2004 it has registered over 1,000 farmers for the programme and has provided advice to nearly 300 farmers.

5.29   The local authority will need to be very clear which local indicators it intends to pursue, the actions or policies it will implement to achieve this and why in applying for LEGI resources.

> **Question 5.5:** How can we ensure the LEGI creates the right balance between indicators, actions and targets?

Integrate efforts   **5.30**   Enterprise development should be part of a wider strategy – encompassed by the Community Strategy – including public service delivery, neighbourhood renewal, and labour supply-side interventions. Where possible, **the local authority should try to capitalise on the obvious synergies between different strategies and, where appropriate, pool resources to make a bigger impact.** The use of LAAs where they exist will provide the flexibility to achieve this.

> **Question 5.6:** What is the best way to ensure that the LEGI is integrated with and generates leverage from other related programmes?

Agree targets   **5.31**   Ultimately, the Government Offices will enter into a negotiation with local authorities that have applied for LEGI funding – and have been successful – to agree what will be delivered for the resources, and what outcome targets are appropriate. **The local enterprise development proposals should clearly suggest appropriate outcome-focused targets and clear milestones over time in return for LEGI support.**

> **Question 5.7:** How detailed should local targets be, and to what extent should they include timed, output measures?

COMMITMENT OF RESOURCES

Long-term commitment

5.32   The LEGI will be worth £50 million in 2006-2007, rising to £150 per year by 2008-2009, subject to confirmation in the 2006 Spending Review. **Local authorities that receive support from the LEGI can expect a long-term commitment of resources – from five to ten years – and should make clear in their applications the long-term timetable for their local proposals.**

5.33   However, the LEGI will not resource proposals that do not focus on the fundamentals required to make a lasting change, or that target unsustainable projects that will need continued support beyond the life of the LEGI. **Local authorities will therefore need to consider at the outset how best to invest the resources for the term of their proposals to ensure the benefits are felt long after the life of the LEGI.** LAA should provide local authorities with the flexibility to integrate this within a wider approach to economic development and neighbourhood renewal.

> **Question 5.8:** How long should funding be available for? How can we ensure that support is time-limited in an effective way that allows local authorities the ability to plan beyond the life of the LEGI?

Resourcing local plans

5.34 Evidence from international experience (such as the US Empowerment Zones), together with evaluation of past UK policies, suggests that the average cost of successful local enterprise development programmes is in the order of **£5 million per deprived area per year.** Obviously this figure will vary depending on the size of the area, the scale of the problem and the types of intervention pursued locally – and this figure should be viewed as a 'middle-case' only. **However, local proposals will be considered and assessed by Government Offices on their merits.**

> **Question 5.9:** What is the critical mass of funding required to make a difference to enterprise in deprived areas? Bear in mind that the greater the level of funding to individual authorities, the less areas can be supported.

5.35 The Government also recognises that it can take considerable time and resources to build local partnerships and develop local proposals in the first place. Some local authorities will be more advanced than others in developing existing proposals for enterprise development. Therefore, the Government is providing £10 million during 2005-2006 divided between all local authorities designated as Neighbourhood Renewal Fund Areas to pump-prime the development of local proposals. This money will not be issued until summer 2005.

Phasing the LEGI

5.36 In addition to pump-priming the development of local proposals, the resources from **the LEGI will be phased in three rounds each worth £50 million per year, starting in 2006-2007.** This would provide extra lead-in time for those local authorities that at present are less advanced in planning economic and enterprise development. This phasing of resources will also allow Government Offices and local authorities to learn from earlier rounds. **Local authorities should therefore not rush to secure funding from round one, but rather should take time to ensure their local proposals are right.**

HOW IT WILL WORK

5.37 The LEGI will not be able to resource all local authorities that are eligible for support. There will therefore be demand for support from the LEGI that the available resources will not be able to meet. The LEGI will therefore operate through an allocation mechanism, where those eligible local authorities with the most developed and thought-through local proposals are more likely to receive financial support. The use of phased rounds of funding will allow those authorities that are unsuccessful in earlier rounds to re-apply in later rounds.

5.38 There are two stages to the division of the LEGI resources: first, between the English regions; and second, between deprived local areas. **The Government will determine the appropriate regional allocation of the LEGI in discussion with the Government Offices and the RDAs.** This allocation will necessarily reflect the geographical variation in levels of deprivation.

Local allocation

5.39   The allocation mechanism will operate through criteria that are clear about both which local authority areas are eligible to apply for LEGI support, and on what criteria eligible local authorities will be assessed.

Eligibility   **5.40**   The key driver of eligibility is deprivation. **The LEGI will not create a new area designation that is determined at the national level.** Rather, it will provide discretion to the local area to determine which area is targeted – based on level of deprivation and enterprise potential – that will fit with existing area based initiatives in the locality.

5.41   **Local areas will have to meet the basic eligibility criteria that they will have to be one of the Neighbourhood Renewal Fund areas. The local authority should also consider the enterprise potential of the area, as this will also be considered by the Government Offices when assessing applications for LEGI support.**

Application   **5.42**   The local authority should then submit its local enterprise development proposals to their Government Office. The Government Office will provide guidance on how to apply for LEGI support.

> **Question 5.10: Is application guidance necessary, and if so, what sort of issues should it cover?**

Selection   **5.43**   **Selection of local deprived areas that will benefit from LEGI support will follow an assessment by the Government Offices – in consultation with the RDAs – on the quality and sustainability of the proposals submitted.** Government Offices are likely to consider the issues outlined previously in this chapter, and may decide to issue a basic and simple set of criteria to guide local authorities.

> **Question 5.11: What elements should form the basis of a fair selection criteria at the regional level?**

Institutional roles   **5.44**   The LEGI will **make use of existing institutional roles and responsibilities.** Figure 5.2 below provides a basic diagrammatic representation of the key roles and stages in the new side-heading LEGI process.

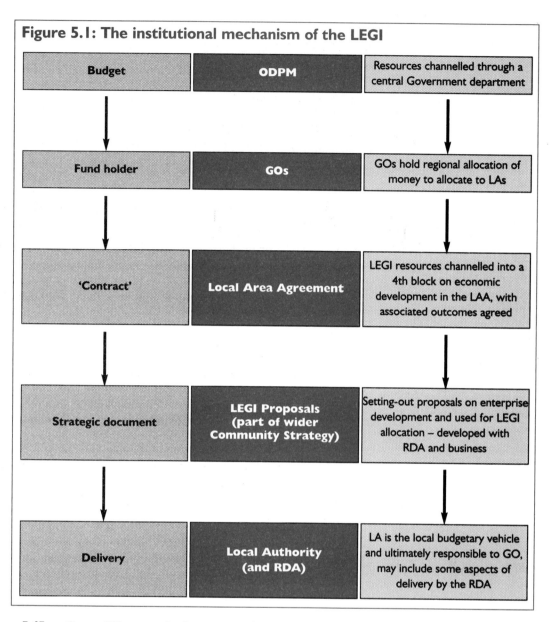

Figure 5.1: The institutional mechanism of the LEGI

Budget	ODPM	Resources channelled through a central Government department
Fund holder	GOs	GOs hold regional allocation of money to allocate to LAs
'Contract'	Local Area Agreement	LEGI resources channelled into a 4th block on economic development in the LAA, with associated outcomes agreed
Strategic document	LEGI Proposals (part of wider Community Strategy)	Setting-out proposals on enterprise development and used for LEGI allocation – developed with RDA and business
Delivery	Local Authority (and RDA)	LA is the local budgetary vehicle and ultimately responsible to GO, may include some aspects of delivery by the RDA

5.45   Care will be exercised to ensure the LEGI process remains simple and intuitive, and is free from unnecessary bureaucracy. The use of LAAs should assist in streamlining the process.

Question 5.12: What are the common aspects of funding of this sort that create unnecessary bureaucratic burdens that the LEGI should try to avoid?

TIMETABLE

Launch of Local Enterprise Growth Initiative

5.46   Research into previous policies has shown that an overly compressed timeframe in which to develop sustainable and robust proposals by those responsible for delivery can have negative impacts on the success and value for money of the policy. As mentioned previously, the LEGI will address this in two ways: first, by operating through three rounds of funding, allowing the more advanced to apply first and providing others with more time for development; and second, by pump-priming the development of local proposals during 2005-2006.

5.47   **The LEGI itself will be launched during 2006-2007, to fit in with the broader timetable set by the ODPM Five Year Plan** *Sustainable Communities: People, Places and Prosperity* .[4]

Consultation

5.48   Prior to the launch of the fund, the Government wishes to formally consult with key stakeholders. This is the purpose of this consultation document, and details of next steps in the consultation are set-out in Chapter 6.

5.49   Following consultation, the process for introducing LEGI would involve the following stages:

- publication of final details of the new fund;

- development of criteria / guidance and putting necessary institutional systems in place;

- building partnerships and coalitions with business by local authorities;

- development of local proposals for sustainable enterprise, investment and economic development by local authorities in partnership with businesses and RDAs;

- assessment of local proposals by Government Offices; and

- negotiation of details and terms of LEGI funding for successful local authorities.

5.50   **Regional institutions and local authorities should therefore begin to prepare as soon as possible for both the introduction of the LEGI, and the invitation to apply for LEGI resources.** However, while eligible local authorities should start to develop proposals soon, they should not submit anything to the Government Offices until requested to do so.

---

[4] Office of the Deputy Prime Minister (2005).

6 NEXT STEPS

6.1   Chapter 4 set-out a series of principles that guided the development of the proposal for a Local Enterprise Growth Initiative (LEGI), set-out in Chapter 5. Chapter 5 asked a series of questions to inform the further development of the fund.

6.2   The Government would welcome the views of all stakeholders on the questions raised in this consultation document. The list of specific questions is reproduced in full below.

6.3   Consultation responses should be sent, by Wednesday 8 June 2005, to:

Local Enterprise Growth Initiative Consultation

Office of the Deputy Prime Minister

Eland House

Bressenden Place

London SW1E 5DU

6.4   The results of the consultation will be published in summer 2005. Consultation responses received after the 8 June deadline may not be considered. Contributions made to the consultation will be anonymised if they are quoted in any public documentation, but stakeholders should state clearly in their response if they do not want to be included in a list of those who have responded.

6.5   The full list of questions for consultation is:

1.   Are the suggested indicators for the LEGI the right ones – are there others to consider? What can be, or is already, measured at the local level that can be used in this way?

2.   In areas without Local Area Agreements, what is the best way to ensure that the LEGI is integrated with and generates leverage from other programmes?

3.   What is the best way of involving local partners in developing local LEGI proposals? How could the Local Strategic Partnerships ensure sufficient business involvement in the development of local proposals for enterprise development and growth?

4.   How can the LEGI best co-ordinate and consolidate evidence and lessons learnt from the resources used?

5.   How can we ensure the LEGI creates the right balance between indicators, actions and targets?

6.   What is the best way to ensure that the LEGI is integrated with and generates leverage from other related programmes?

7.   How detailed should local targets be, and to what extent should they include timed, output measures?

8.   How long should funding be available for? How can we ensure that support is time-limited in an effective way that allows local authorities the ability to plan beyond the life of the LEGI?

9.   What is the critical mass of funding required to make a difference to enterprise in deprived areas? Bear in mind that the greater the level of funding to individual authorities, the less areas can be supported.

10. Is application guidance necessary, and if so, what sort of issues should it cover?

11. What elements should form the basis of a fair selection criteria at the regional level?

12. What are the common aspects of funding of this sort that create unnecessary bureaucratic burdens that the LEGI should try to avoid?

ENTERPRISE AREAS

AI   Enterprise and economic activity are central to the Government's actions to tackle poverty, unemployment and social exclusion. The Enterprise Areas announced in 2002 Pre-Budget Report aim to help address the range of barriers to enterprise, economic activity and opportunity for all, and draw-together the range of policy tools available to local and regional organisations to tackle the problems their communities face.

Enterprise Areas – definition

"Enterprise Areas provide a flexible range of policies which [local authorities] can promote to tackle the barriers to enterprise that exist in deprived wards."

(John Healey MP, Economic Secretary to the Treasury, 2003)

A2   The Enterprise Areas are the 1,997 most deprived areas of the UK. In England, Wales and Northern Ireland the areas are defined at ward level using the relevant indices of deprivation. In Scotland, the areas are defined using postcode sectors.

A3   In England and Scotland the areas selected are the most deprived 15 per cent of wards/areas, in Wales and Northern Ireland they are the most deprived 42 per cent of wards to reflect higher levels of deprivation in these countries.[1] In England, 73 per cent of them lie within the 88 local authorities which receive support from the Neighbourhood Renewal Fund and in which the most deprived neighbourhoods are concentrated.

---

[1] The Enterprise Areas were selected using the Index of Multiple Deprivation 2000 (England); the Welsh Index of Multiple Deprivation 2000; the Scottish Area Deprivation Index 1998; and the Northern Ireland Measures of Deprivation 2001.

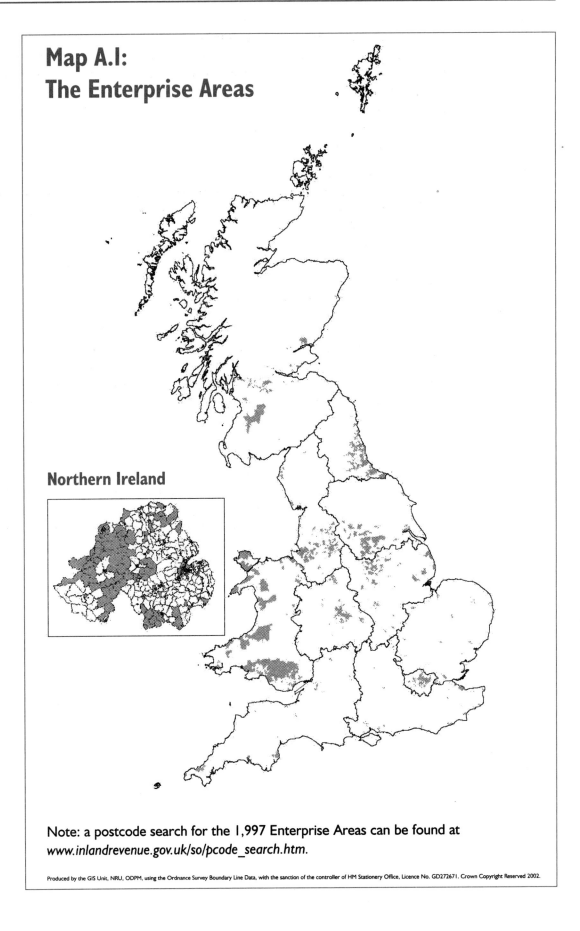

Map A.I:
The Enterprise Areas

Northern Ireland

Note: a postcode search for the 1,997 Enterprise Areas can be found at
www.inlandrevenue.gov.uk/so/pcode_search.htm.

Produced by the GIS Unit, NRU, ODPM, using the Ordnance Survey Boundary Line Data, with the sanction of the controller of HM Stationery Office, Licence No. GD272671. Crown Copyright Reserved 2002.

A4   Local authorities and Local Strategic Partnerships – together with their regional development agencies (RDAs) – have a significant role to play in using the opportunities presented by these measures to support and strengthen their own strategies for economic development and local regeneration, and in boosting the awareness and uptake of relevant local measures by local businesses. The way in which RDAs, local authorities and other regional and local partners take-up and deploy these measures can and should vary to reflect varying local circumstances.

A5   For example, take-up of business support and external finance can vary significantly between cultural and social groups for a variety of reasons. In some areas it may be more appropriate to tackle these issues through introducing or supporting a targeted businesses support programme, designed to overcome an unwillingness or reluctance to approach mainstream sources of advice or finance – drawing on the lessons of the Phoenix Fund – while in other areas it might require the establishment of a Community Development Finance Institution (CDFI), able to provide tailored finance packages to those who find it difficult to access bank finance. In other areas, the use of planning flexibilities to reduce barriers to the start-up or expansion of local businesses may be of greater importance.

A6   Supporting enterprise in deprived areas is a vital part of the Government's wider neighbourhood renewal objectives. As such, the Government committed to developing the approach taken through the Enterprise Areas package as evaluation, research, and experience at the local level provide further evidence on the scale of market failures and the effectiveness of policy.

Enterprise Areas – policy measures

A7   Table A.1 shows how current interventions tackle the market failures and barriers to enterprise that can be most severe in Enterprise Areas, but the Government would value further evidence from local and regional partners on the further steps that could be taken to tackle the problems highlighted.

Table A.1: Current interventions in Enterprise Areas

Barriers and market failures in Enterprise Areas	Policy measure(s) targeted at this barrier/failure
Greater difficulties in accessing finance	Community Investment Tax Relief
	Bridges Community Development Venture Fund
	Support for Community Development Finance Institutions
Property market failures, and low levels of private sector investment	Business Premises Renovation Allowance
	Business Planning Zones
	Package of measures to help local authorities improve the planning system
	Contaminated land tax credit
	Other urban regeneration fiscal measures
	Tax incentive to encourage business donations towards the running costs of Urban Regeneration Companies
Lack of suitable business premises	Higher feasibility grants from the Business Incubation Fund in the 20% most disadvantaged areas of England
Need for targeted business support and advice, and enterprise outreach to raise skills and awareness of opportunities, and to tackle cultural barriers	Business Links have targets on the take-up of business support in disadvantaged areas
	Projects funded by the Phoenix Development Fund
	Support from HM Revenue and Customs
	Dedicated section in the *No-Nonsense Guide to Government rules and regulations for setting up your business*
	Enterprise Advisers for schools
	New Entrepreneur Scholarships

Access to finance A8 **Community Investment Tax Relief**, to improve access to finance for small business and social enterprise by opening-up new markets for commercial lending through CDFIs.

A9 CDFIs provide finance to businesses excluded from mainstream finance, operating mainly in disadvantaged areas. The credit provides tax relief worth 25 per cent of capital over five years to individuals and corporations who invest in or lend to a qualifying CDFI. Details of accredited CDFIs are available on the Small Business Service (SBS) website (www.sbs.gov.uk).

A10 The **Bridges Community Development Venture Fund**, a £40 million fund made up of investment from Government and the private sector, to provide venture capital funding to firms in the 25 per cent most disadvantaged areas of England that can demonstrate meaningful interaction with the local economy.

A11 **Support to CDFIs** through the Phoenix Fund – further details are provided below.

Property market failures A12 The Government is implementing a package of planning measures to help local authorities speed-up and simplify the planning process in Enterprise Areas in England, including:

- guidance for **Business Planning Zones**, which will give Local Authorities the power to designate zones in which there is no requirement to apply for planning permission where predetermined criteria are met;

- setting aside resources from the Planning Delivery Grant to assist authorities delivering planning for Enterprise Areas, from 2004-2005;

- encouraging local authorities to use Local Development Orders in Enterprise Areas and, subject to forthcoming guidance, granting automatic planning permission for types of development specified in such Orders; and

- working with local authorities to ensure Enterprise Areas are effectively planned for in local plans.

AI3 Fiscal measures to support urban regeneration, available in all areas of the UK:

- a 150 per cent accelerated payable tax credit for the costs of cleaning-up contaminated land;

- 100 per cent first-year capital allowances for creating flats over shops and other commercial premises for letting; and

- targeted VAT reductions to encourage the renovation of existing residential properties and their conversion into multiple dwellings.

AI4 A tax incentive to encourage business donations toward the running costs of Urban Regeneration Companies (URCs), including those operating in Enterprise Areas. The tax incentive allows businesses to deduct expenditure on contributions, whether in cash or in kind, toward the running costs of URCs when computing their taxable profits.

Business premises **AI5** Grants for business incubators have been awarded to cover the costs of feasibility studies for incubators in England, with higher levels of funding in the 88 neighbourhood renewal areas that are also Enterprise Areas. Grants of up to £30,000, to cover up to 70 per cent of the cost of the study, were available in disadvantaged areas. In other areas, grants of up to £20,000 were offered to cover 50 per cent of the cost of the study.

Business support **AI6** The Phoenix Fund, which is designed to encourage enterprise in disadvantaged areas and communities. It consists of two main parts; a Development Fund, which promotes innovative ways of supporting enterprise in deprived areas, and support to Community Development Finance Institutions (through a Challenge Fund to help resource CDFIs, and a loan guarantee scheme to encourage commercial and charitable lending to them).

AI7 Enhanced support from HM Revenue and Customs in Enterprise Areas through their Business Support Teams, EmployerTalk events and Business Advice Open Days.

AI8 The New Entrepreneur Scholarship programme (NES) helps individuals living in Enterprise Areas to start in business by providing a comprehensive package of support, mentoring and funding in order to encourage and support the start-up and growth of new businesses.

AI9 Funding to provide Enterprise Advisers for schools in disadvantaged areas of England, particularly in the Enterprise Areas, to work alongside headteachers in around 1,000 secondary schools to encourage enterprise practice among teachers and pupils.

A22 The Government believes there is yet more that could be done to further strengthen the Enterprise Areas package, thereby helping to close the enterprise gap, and develop the local economies of deprived areas – with local authorities and RDAs determining measures appropriate for their areas.

B ACKNOWLEDGEMENTS

The Local Enterprise Growth Initiative project team spoke to a large number of stakeholders within local and regional institutions, businesses and business organisations, academics, third sector organisations, as well as international officials and academics. These discussions were extremely useful in helping to shape the proposal outlined in this document, but it should be noted that the views expressed in this document are those of central government and may not be the views of stakeholders spoken to. We are very grateful for everyone who gave their time and valuable assistance and would particularly like to mention the following:

- all those who participated in an expert seminar on *Enterprise and regeneration of deprived areas*, with particular thanks to the speakers and chairs of the event;

- the Innovation Forum of excellent local authorities who met to provide a local authority perspective on local enterprise and regeneration;

- all those who participated in a seminar organised by the Countryside Agency on *Enterprise and regeneration of disadvantaged areas – a rural perspective*, with particular thanks to the speakers and to the Countryside Agency for hosting the event;

- regional development agencies and Government Offices who have been involved in various events and meetings, as well as helping to organise visits;

- business organisations including Business Links, Chambers of Commerce, and ethnic minority organisations who participated in events and hosted meetings with businesses;

- the local organisations who provided case studies to use in this document; and

- a particular thanks to all the businesses that used their valuable time to participate in events and meetings.

C

REFERENCES

Annie E. Casey Foundation (2002): Voices from the empowerment zones – insights about launching large-scale community revitalization initiatives.

Audretsch, D. & Thurik, R. (2001): Linking entrepreneurship to growth, STI *working paper*, OECD.

Bank of England (2000): Finance for small businesses in deprived communities – a first report.

Business in the Community on behalf of the Department of Trade and Industry (2002): business investment in under-served markets: an opportunity for businesses communities?

Business in the Community (2005): Under-served Markets – Preliminary research findings.

Cabinet Office (2001): A New Commitment to Neighbourhood Renewal – National Strategy Action Plan – A report by the Social Exclusion Unit.

Dale, I. & Morgan, A. (2001): Job creation – the role of new and small firms, *Small Business Service / TRENDS Business Research*.

Department of the Environment (1993): City Challenge: interim national evaluation.

Department of the Environment, Transport and the Regions (2000): Final Evaluation of City Challenge, *Regeneration Research*.

Department of Trade and Industry (2002a): Productivity and competitiveness indicators update 2002.

Department of Trade and Industry (2002b): Social Enterprise: a strategy for success.

Educe Ltd CEA on behalf of Office of the Deputy Prime Minister, Home Office, Department of Trade and Industry, and Business in the Community (2005): Brokering Business Connections – engaging business support for neighbourhood renewal: Summary evaluation of the Business Brokers Pilot Programme

European Commission (2003): Green Paper – Entrepreneurship in Europe.

Global Entrepreneurship Monitor (2003): 2003 Executive Report.

Global Entrepreneurship Monitor (2004): United Kingdom report 2004, Rebecca Harding.

GHK (2003): Evaluation of City Growth Strategies (CGS) – Stage One Report to the Small Business Service.

GHK (2004): Evaluation of City Growth Strategies (CGS) – Final Report to the Small Business Service.

HM Government (2002): Cross-cutting review of government services for small business.

HM Treasury (1999): Enterprise and social exclusion, *National Strategy for Neighbourhood Renewal: Policy Action Team 3*.

HM Treasury (2000): Productivity in the UK: The Evidence and the Government's Approach.

HM Treasury (2001a): Reforming Britain's economic and financial policy: towards greater economic stability, *Palgrave*.

HM Treasury (2001b): Productivity in the UK: Enterprise and the Productivity Challenge.

HM Treasury (2001c): Productivity in the UK: Progress towards a productive economy.

HM Treasury (2001d): Enterprising Communities: A tax incentive for community investment – A consultation document.

HM Treasury (2004a): Promoting financial inclusion.

HM Treasury (2004b): 2004 Spending Review.

HM Treasury (2004c): Spending Review 2004 – Public Service Agreements White Paper.

HM Treasury (2004d): Reducing administrative burdens: effective inspection and enforcement, Philip Hampton.

HM Treasury/ Department of Trade and Industry (2001): Productivity in the UK: 3 – The Regional Dimension.

HM Treasury/Small Business Service (2002): Enterprise Britain: a modern approach to meeting the enterprise challenge.

HM Treasury/Small Business Service (2003): Bridging the finance gap: a consultation on improving access to growth capital for small business.

HM Treasury/Office of the Deputy Prime Minister (2003): Productivity in the UK: 4 – The Local Dimension.

HM Treasury/Cabinet Office (2004): Devolving decision making: 1 – Delivering better public services: refining targets and performance management.

HM Treasury/Department of Trade and Industry/Office of the Deputy Prime Minister (2004): Devolving decision making: 2 – Meeting the regional economic challenge: Increasing regional and local flexibility.

HM Treasury/Home Office/ Department of Trade and Industry (2005): Exploring the role of the third sector in public service delivery and reform – A discussion document.

Kempson, E. & Mackinnon, K. (2002): Self-employment in deprived communities, Personal Finance Research Centre.

Local Government Association (2003): Economic regeneration – documenting best practice.

Local Government Association (2004): Independence, opportunity, trust – a manifesto for local communities.

Local Government Association/Improvement and Development Agency (2003): supporting local business – what can we learn from the beacons?

London School of Economics (2003): Is Targeting Deprived Areas an Effective Means to Reach Poor People? An assessment of one rationale for area-based funding programmes, Centre for Analysis of Social Exclusion.

Lord Trotman (2000): Review of Government Measures for Enterprise Growth: A Report by Lord Trotman.

Loveman, G. & Sengenberger, W. (1991): The re-emergence of small-scale production: an international comparison, Small Business Economics, Vol. 3, pp.1-37.

New Economics Foundation (2004): The Inner City 100: impacts and influences,

Office of the Deputy Prime Minister (2003): Transferable Lessons from Enterprise Zones – Urban Research Summary Number 12, 2003.

Office of the Deputy Prime Minister (2004a): Jobs and Enterprise in Deprived Areas – a Social Exclusion Unit Report.

Office of the Deputy Prime Minister (2004b): Local Area Agreements: a prospectus.

Office of the Deputy Prime Minister (2004c): The future of local government: Developing a ten year vision.

Office of the Deputy Prime Minister (2005): Sustainable Communities: People, Places and Prosperity.

Office of the Deputy Prime Minister/Small Business Service (2003): Research Report 5 – Business-led regeneration of deprived areas – A review of the evidence base.

OECD (1998): Fostering Entrepreneurship – Policy Brief no.9, 1998.

OECD (2001): Science, technology and industry outlook, drivers of growth: information technology, innovation and entrepreneurship.

OECD (2003a): Entrepreneurship and Local Economic Development – Programme and policy recommendations.

OECD (2003b): Financing Entrepreneurship in Distressed Areas – presentation by Diane C. Lupke, CecD.

Reynolds, P., Bygrave, W., Autio, E., Cox, L. & Hay, M. (2002): Global entrepreneurship monitor 2002 executive report.

Scarpetta, S., Hemmings, P., Tressel, T. & Woo, J. (2002): The role of policy and institutions for productivity and firm dynamics: evidence from micro and industry data, *OECD Working Paper 329.*

Social Investment Task Force (2000): Enterprising communities: wealth beyond welfare – A report to the Chancellor of the Exchequer from the Social Investment Task Force.

Small Business Service (2002): Measuring enterprise impacts in deprived areas – full report and executive summary.

Small Business Service (2003a): A government action plan for small business – Making the UK the best place in the world to start and grow a business.

Small Business Service (2003b): A government action plan for small business – The evidence base.

Small Business Service (2004a): Household Survey of Entrepreneurship 2003 – Full report and Executive Summary.

Small Business Service (2004b): Annual Small Business Survey 2003 – Executive Summary.

Small Business Service/ICIC (2003): City Growth Strategy – A New Agenda for Business-led Urban Regeneration.

The Beta Model Limited (2004): Enterprise Dynamics in the 20 per cent Most Deprived Wards in England, Garry Haywood & Jeremy Nicholls.

The Northern Way Steering Group (2004): Moving Forward: The Northern Way: First Growth Strategy Report.

Trends Business Research (2001): Business Clusters in the UK – A First Assessment – Volume 1 Main Report.

US Department of Housing and Urban Development (2001): Interim Assessment of the Empowerment Zones and Enterprise Communities (EZ/EC) Program: A Progress Report.

Welsh Development Agency (2004): Cyfenter Transnational Research Report – Encouraging Self-Employment through the State Benefit and Tax Systems.